W9-AWL-101

WHAT READERS ARE SAYING:

In *Your True DNA*, Thom Winninger grapples with questions many people are afraid to ask and even fewer can answer. Find out who you are, why you are here, and God's best for you.

Mark Sanborn, President Sanborn & Associates and author of *The Fred Factor and The Potential Principle*

Thom Winninger's book is not just an engaging read, it's an essential companion to support your life journey. I had no idea how much I needed his profound wisdom and practical insights to help me realize more of my potential. Perhaps most importantly, it can help you overcome burnout from the chaos of your daily life. It has given me clarity and momentum at a critical inflection point in my life. Buy it, keep it close and get ready to realize your true purpose.

Manley Feinberg II, Author of *Reaching Your Next Summit*, Founder and CEO of Vertical Lessons, Inc.

Inspiring and personally applicable! *Your True DNA* is about more than doing — it is about being. So many books are about the goal — this one is about the journey — the much more important eternal journey. Thank you Thom, for this gift.

David Horsager, MA, Author of *The Trust Edge*

In *Your True DNA*, Thom not only guides you on how to truly ask the question "What?" he also skillfully guides you on creating your own journey to discover the "How." An amazing read to find your gift and impact the lives of those around you.

Mark Scharenbroich, Author of *Nice Bike — Making Meaningful Connections on the Road of Life.*

"The unexamined life is not worth living" so stated Socrates. It behooves all of us to think before acting. Yet, how many of us really take time to identify our life's purpose? In "Your True DNA" Winninger gives us direction and reason to determine our path toward a life of fulfillment."

Jim Tunney, Ed.D. Former NFL
Referee, Author, Speaker

Your True DNA not only draws upon philosophical wisdom, but also psychological insights and personal experience. Thom provides a trustworthy map guiding you to deeper meaning, freedom and joy. Discover your Divinely-Intended Gift.

Rob Kroll SJ, Retreat Master,
teacher Creighton University Prep

Oh… to open the pages of Thom's amazing book is comparable to being given the golden key to your life's mystery maze. You will identify at once with the grateful man who cried out, "I once was blind, but now I see."

Glenna Salsbury, CSP, CPAE, committed believer,
Author of *The Art of the Fresh Start*

Acorns that try to become redwoods are always frustrated and unsuccessful. You were created for a purpose. Once you discover your true calling, your DNA, then life will thrive in you. Thom Winninger, my mentor and friend, will show you how."

Jim Cathcart, Author of
The Acorn Principle

"DNA, your Divine Natural Attribute, is not just a book, it is a movement of those seeking purpose, meaning, and joy in their lives. No matter your faith orientation, this book will lead you to the Divine Intent for *your* life!"

LeAnn Thieman, Author
Chicken Soup for the Soul, a Book of Miracles

This book is truly needed in today's superficial, frenetic, and distracted world. Thom Winninger helps us find an inner path to the divine truth of our purpose, meaning, serenity, and joy. Very timely and inspiring!

Christian Ellis, Leadership Adviser and
Executive Coach Author of
The Enlightened Enterprise

Building on insightful thoughts, the irrefutable transparency of Truth so resonates in your soul, desired transformation is the outcome. *Your True DNA* is a Treatise for the ages.

Francis Bologna, Managing Dir.
Francis Bologna and Assoc.

Thom Winninger has captured the soul of the Gift, the heart of the Call and the path of Divine Intent. What an adventure of self-discovery! Delve into 'Your True DNA' and you will see yourself and your life through an exciting new lens.

Elizabeth Jeffries, Executive Leadership Coach
and Author of *Breakthrough Coaching*

While man has continually searched for meaning, Thom Winninger leads you on a viable path of self-discovery that leads to a life of meaning, purpose, fulfillment and joy.

Dan Janal, President, PR Leads Author,
Reporters Are Looking for YOU!

All of us share one common desire in life, to find fulfillment in what we do and in our lives. Yet often we are so consumed in our search for success we often find fulfillment ellusive. *Your True DNA* will guide you through a spiritual journey on how to find and use your inner gift to achieve your ultimate goal... fulfillment.

Ron Karr, Author
Lead, Sell or Get Out of the Way!

The 12 Truths alone make this *Your True DNA* worth reading not to mention the passages to discover God's Gift within you.

Stacy Tetschner, Former CEO,
National Speakers Assoc.

Having experienced Winninger's teaching style this book is a class well-taught, rooted in his own journey, and enhanced by the thought of theologians and philosophers. Your walk through life will be motivated by this essay on self-discovery and application of one's gifts.

Dr. Lynn Trapp, author,
liturgical musician

Thom has shared the "noting" of his life journey, since a 2001 "wake up call", with succinct, passionate articulation. The "true DNA" placed within us by a Sovereign God is a gift to realize "who we are" for the benefit of others, and service to Him.

Naomi Rhode, CSP, CPAE,
Co-Founder SmartPractice

Winninger has been a source of inspiration and wisdom for me for the past 30 years. His newest book, *Your True DNA*, takes that wisdom to a whole new level that has caused me to look in the mirror and ask more significant questions.

Stephen Tweed, CSP, CEO,
Leading Home Care — Tweed Jeffries company

Thom's offers a compelling invitation to better understand your true "DNA" — our Divine Natural God given Attribute. Thom channels God's unrelenting optimism for each of us and joyfully offers the challenge and blessing of choosing to become "Big Believers".

Arthur A. Pingolt, Jr., President,
Missionary Oblate Partnership

Intellectually sound...Spiritually nourishing...Thom's new book *Your True DNA* is a winner!

Tim Murray, Adjunct Professor and
Executive Director at Trinity Sober Homes

Winninger is one of the best and brightest thinkers on this earth. *Your True DNA* will empower your thoughts and inspire your actions to help you do more, be more and achieve more! Read it you will be glad you did!"

Dr. Willie Jolley — Best Selling
Author of *A Setback Is A Setup*

Your True DNA: Discovering God's Gift Within You is a guidebook for complete transformation—discovering what God always intended for you and me. Thank you, Thom Winninger for helping light the way.

Phillip Van Hooser, Author of *Leaders Ought To Know: 11 Ground Rules for Common Sense Leadership*

Winninger reminds us of the ancient wisdom that finding meaning and purpose in life requires us to find our Gift, our true DNA. Filled with practical insights and personal experience, *Your True DNA* will speak to anyone who asks: What am I to do with my life?

Robert G Kennedy, PhD Professor, Department of Catholic Studies, University of St. Thomas

A life changing transformational book. Thom does a brilliant deep dive job of revealing how to discover your true DNA (Divine Natural Attribute), your GIFT vs your skills or strengths. A must read if you are looking for true joy, meaning, satisfaction and fulfillment in your life!

Kathy B. Dempsey, RN MED CSP, President, Keep Shedding! Inc. Founder, The Shedding Revolution! Transformational Results!

There is a joy and peace that comes from realizing we are perfectly made—made in God's image with unique gifts and talents to serve Him and others. This book is a beautiful companion on the journey to discerning your unique gifts and God's plan for you.

Julie Ditter, Accenture

Your True
DNA

YOUR TRUE DNA

DISCOVERING GOD'S GIFT WITHIN YOU!

THOMAS J. WINNINGER

ST. THOMAS PRESS

St. Thomas Press
5637 Interlachen Circle
Minneapolis, MN 55436
612.801.3194
www.winninger.com

© 2017 by Thomas J. Winninger

All rights reserved. No part of this publication may be reproduced, stored in a retrieval system, or transmitted, in any form or by any means, electronic, mechanical, photocopying, recording, or otherwise, without the prior written permission of the author.

All Scriptures are taken from the New American Bible Revised Edition, 2011 Oxford University Press.

Printed in the United States of America

ISBN13: 978-0-96387-355-2
LCCN: 2017950919

CONTENTS

DON'T KID YOURSELF

D on't kid yourself. Each of us will come to a point in our life sooner or later, when we realize that something is missing. We come to a recognition that there are unanswered questions, and things don't seem to be working out the way we expected. On the sooner side, we have graduated from college with a degree that we thought would lead to a successful career. Whether it did or not, we aren't finding life to be what we expected. We want meaning and fulfillment – a belief that our life will make a difference – but most of what we find is a grind without a bigger purpose than just getting things done. On the later end of the scale, we may have put in many years of work, successful or not, and have discovered much the same thing. There are those of us who have attained a level of financial stability, or there may be those of us who have limited accomplishments and questionable financial security; both situations can produce "no fulfillment or meaning." It is intriguing that we all arrive eventually having the same need. You ask, "Well, what happened to the group between the sooner and the later ends?" Well, they are just so busy trying to build a career or stuck in a rut in their life that they have impaired their ability to hear. It may take something bigger than this message to get their attention. In some unfortunate

1

cases, it takes a physical, financial, mental, or spiritual calamity that cannot be understood or explained in human terms, to bring them to the more important questions in life.

Who am I?
What is the purpose of my life?
What am I going to do with the rest of my life?
Why is there so much tension in my daily life?
Why do I feel stuck, unhappy, frustrated, and unsatisfied?
Why am I working so hard but emotionally so disconnected?
Why do I feel like the world is passing me by?
Why is there no clarity or direction in my life?
Why are my relationships not working?
Why didn't I get the job out of school that I prepared for?
Why haven't things turned out the way I had planned?
Why do I feel unappreciated?

If you come to a point in your life when these questions are yelling at you, it is not time to grab a bunch of books on the subject or meaning of life. It is not time to call up your friends and acquaintances to have a cup of coffee or lunch and ask them for their advice as to what you should be doing with your life. Take note that they — most of them, anyway — are asking the same questions and not getting any answers, either. It is not the time to quit your job or dump your relationships because you think you need to buy a hut in Turks and Caicos to escape from the tension in your life. I guarantee that after a few days in that hut by yourself, you will come to the tragic realization that you took the problem with you, and the real problem is you. I also guarantee the solution to your confusion is also you; it is in you; it is in what I have referred to as your D.N.A. (Divine Natural Attribute — Your Gift) Now is the time to truly get to know who you are rather than try to escape yourself.

The insights of this work are the result of over sixty years of life on this earth, which include fifteen years of work in individual and organizational purposing. In these years, it has become very clear to me that what we call the journey is more a path of life than a journey. This path is made up of ideas and truths; however, in many cases, they are not convergent. In other words, most ideas are not supported by a truth; ideas are generated by human desires, wants, and passions. Be assured that ideas that are convergent with truths make the all the difference in answering the questions stated above about life. You see, when ideas are connected with truths, those ideas are sustaining and, if followed, will bring you to find your fuller potential. They will bring you to making the world a better place.

One basic truth is, "We are not made for work; work is made for us." In other words, "Who we are" is not determined by what we do, not by our work. "Who we are" is determined by how we apply our innate Gift and talents in all we do. Because of the misunderstanding of the idea of work, most of us get a job or career but never get a life. A job or career by its very nature does not lead one to a meaningful, satisfying, joy-filled life. If a job or career becomes the main life object, we can be led to an unfulfilled existence of yearning and always wanting more, never getting enough. If you have a meaningful life, it is not the job, career, or relationship, but rather how you found a higher purpose in the job, career, or relationship. Would it not be better to ask people to what purpose are they applying their life rather than simply asking them what they do for a living? Do I have your attention yet? My objective in writing this book is to share what I have discovered about the truths and passages of a life that can be found and applied to its true purpose. It is not only to identify the truths of a purposeful life but to demonstrate how you apply them to find meaning, fulfillment, satisfaction, and joy no matter what you do.

ACKNOWLEDGEMENTS

My deepest thanks to the thousands of people who became my Uncommon Companions during these past sixteen years helping me maintain my own journey of discovering God's Gift within me. Special acknowledgements to Christopher Ellis for his clarity in helping me see God's hand in my daily life, to Candice Dahline and her group of readers whose participation in the discussions of the validity of the Truths in application of real life. To my wife of thirty-seven years, Lynne, whose faith in God and faith in me never faltered. Thank you to my mother and father, Betty and Larry Winninger, who taught me the faith by living it in their own lives. Also, to all those who have prayed for me, confirmed me, inspired me, and held me up when the journey was overwhelming.

Oh Lord, in your great love and mercy you have carried me when I could not carry myself. Help me to continue to unpack truth so others can encounter you in their daily lives, Amen.

WHY ME?

W hen did you fall down? When did you fail? When did you succeed at something you really wanted and devoted your life to achieving? When you did achieve it, why did you feel like it was not enough? Why did you feel like there should have been more? On the morning of Tuesday October 23, 2001, I was in Grapevine, Texas preparing to give a speech to yet another group of dealers about how they need to lead rather than compete. By this time, I had personalized this presentation to over 2,400 groups very similar to this group. This was their annual conference, and I was their keynote speaker.

As I prepared to head down to the conference room at the hotel to check out the audio-visual equipment, I felt weak and had to sit down on the edge of the bed for a minute to catch my breath. As I sat there, all kinds of questions rushed through my mind, like boxcars on a train out of control. The questions I remember most clearly were, "Why are you doing this? "Why are you travelling around from town to town speaking to groups?" "What are you supposed to be doing with your life?" "Where is the meaning in your life?" "Is this just another speech?" "How long can you keep up this journey?" These were just a few of what I felt were among hundreds of similar questions that rushed through my conscious state for which I had no answers, at least not at that moment.

Suddenly, I became flushed, chilled all over, and over-whelmed. I began to cry as I felt my world was completely out of control even though I was at the peak of my career, never better on the platform. I had already completed my bucket list, so to speak. I had a beautiful family and wonderful homes. I had the opportunity to travel various parts of the world and had written five books. I was listed in the Speaker Hall of Fame and had received the Cavett Award from the National Speakers Association as their highest single honor. Despite all of these accomplishments, here I sit on the edge of a bed in a hotel in Grapevine, Texas looking at my watch, trying to remind myself it was time to go do what I do so well, but why and for what?

Needless to say, I did get through the presentation and made my way to the airport where I boarded my flight to Orlando for another speaking engagement the next day. It was on that flight where I reflected on what had really happened that morning before I spoke. I will say it was a wakeup call — an epiphany, so to speak. When reflecting on my life, I realized that I had everything, but at the same time I had nothing. I had accomplished everything but didn't sense the meaning in anything. It kept coming to me like the song, "What Is It All about, Alfie?" written by Burt Bacharach and Hal David for the movie *Alfie*. What is life all about? Is this what I am meant to be doing? Where is the satisfaction in my life? Where is the meaning? These questions kept repeating themselves. They stuck in my head and naturally, being a self-determined person since third grade, I made a commitment on that flight to figure out how to get control of what was happening to me. That was the beginning of what has brought me to where I am today in writing this book. I would have said then, it is what changed my life. Today I say, it is what transformed the reality of my life and brought me meaning, joy, fulfillment, satisfaction, and a legacy of significance.

The first mistake I made was to call my friends and meet with them one by one to ask them the same questions I could not answer myself. "Who am I? What should I be doing? What is life all about?" Immediately, I came to realize they had no idea of what I should be doing, except to remind me that I was very successful, which I did not want to hear. Then I understood; they were in the midst of asking themselves the same questions. How could they help me if they could not even answer these same questions for themselves? Following this false start, something inside of me said to take a break; quit planning and organizing every moment of your day. Quit setting goals and determining future aspirations, at least for a while. That is exactly what I did for the next six months. I just let things happen, dealing with what came my way rather than trying to manage every moment. Again, something inside of me gave me permission to go with the flow. That *something* said to me that what was happening here was bigger than me and would work itself out if I gave it permission to do so. I had been raised by parents who believed in the Divine Nature of life and the when things do not make sense, take it to prayer. Now I was raised a Catholic and attended Catholic schools; I even attended Marquette University in Milwaukee and enjoyed my Jesuit education. These were all good experiences, so at this time in my life I reconnected with my faith. I was regularly attending Mass on Sundays and stopping by the chapel occasionally to find some peace and quiet.

During one of my visits, I wandered into the chapel library to get some reading material to pass the time while enjoying the peacefulness. Feeling overwhelmed as I stared at the wall of books, I noticed a particular thick book sticking out in my face as if someone had shoved it out as I was walking by. I pulled it off the shelf thinking this was too serious of a book to support a few simple minutes of quiet reflection. As

I opened it, my eyes came to rest on the passage beginning with Augustine Confessions, "Late have I loved you, I looked for you everywhere but you were inside of me all the time." It makes no difference if you are of faith or not; Augustine is one of the greatest philosophers of all time because he deals with what I have come to call "street truth"—real-life stuff. He started me on the path that I needed. What I heard him say was, "The answer to the meaning of life is an inside job; getting to know yourself and the meaning of your life is locked inside of you already." Now, I did not understand any of this at the time. Because of that book, *Transformation in Christ*, written by Detrick Von Hildebrand, I came to do three things: First, I started a pattern of reflecting each morning and examining the day each evening. I call it looped-reflection.

Over a short period of time, this determined pattern brought me to a point where things became clearer by simply listening and observing what was happening in my life. Each morning I said a little prayer request—for example, "Help me today to realize my Gift and talents." That evening I would examine what came to me during that day in response to my request, simply asking, "What happened today that helped me to come to know more about my Gift?" After the morning reflection and the evening examination, I would make notes of what came to me. I call it "noting"' The idea is, over a period of, say, thirty days, to identify the consistencies or repetitive messages that come from different questions and experiences. As an example: it came to me that my Gift was insight. In other words, relatively quickly I could take an abstract concept and make it actionable, applicable to everyday circumstances so that people could get better results out of life and work. Second, as a result of the book, I enrolled in a series of classes related to philosophy and theology. I wanted to confirm the origin of Truth, or at least the foundation of Truth. It included Aristotle, Aquinas, Augustine, Karl Rahner, Detrick Von Hildebrand, Catherine of Siena, St. Jerome, and others too numerous to mention. They confirmed in my mind that Truth is not something we own but rather something that owns us. When one lives his or her life with Truth, the meaning of things will become clearer and more obvious. With Truth, one finds that joy does not come from knowing things or having things, but rather from understanding that there is some good that can come from everything. Third, my studies inspired me to apply Truth to all parts of my life, including relationships, work, learning, service, management, leadership, parenting, faith, and even politics. There is no limit to the significance that can come when the foundational Truth becomes the guide post of all living. Don't be confused; Truth embodies character, virtue, justice, and morality. It is true that the wider the gap between Truth and daily life, the more tension there is in life. You see, life is not about change; it is about transformation. It is not about becoming different; it is about becoming the real self. Life is about becoming what you were created to be.

To me, it is about becoming what God created me to be. The path I am on has led me to lead others, both individuals and organizations, to engage the truths in whatever they are doing. It is simply discovering your unique Gift and talents; applying them in such a way that you come to understand your life's purpose, and the call to make the world around you a better place.

On the following pages, I am sharing the summation of the truths that came to me. I will relate how the truths will lead you through the passages of transformation to becoming who you are meant to be and how you can make a choice to transform the rest of your life. You will have the opportunity to discover and live out your fuller potential and purpose. In turn, this will result in finding meaning, fulfillment, and joy. "Engage and live your fuller potential at any cycle of life!"

The answer to, "Why Me?" is "Why Not Me?"..."Why Not You?"

TWELVE TRUTHS OF UNDERSTANDING YOUR REAL SELF

For the sake of your self-discovery, you're becoming what you are meant to be, which will lead you to a life of deeper meaning, purpose, fulfillment, and joy. There are twelve Truths that have disclosed themselves as part of my work. There is no demand at this point that you accept them as Truth, but over time as you seek to know what you're called to do with your life, you will come to accept them as the foundation of self-discovery. In doing so, you will agree to let them prove or disprove themselves. This is the beauty of universal or Absolute Truth. Dr. Michael Naughton, a professor at the University of St. Thomas, once reminded me, "We do not own Truth! Truth owns us!" The wise person will submit to let Truth prove itself for itself over time. It will do this in the application of the Truth. If it is really Truth, the outcomes or fruits will become obvious, for it is true that Truth will triumph in its own right. This is why the writings of Aristotle and Thomas Aquinas continue to be references. We do not need to manage it; we simply need to apply our ideas to it for sustainability. If this book is based on Truth, it will work its way in your life so that you discover yourself, your Gift, your talents, your purpose, your call, your vocation, your career—your *life*.

As we begin, we are not called to seek the answers to the process; we are called to surrender to some basic truths that continue to prove themselves over time. During the past fifteen years of my own personal study, twelve Truths have emerged as the foundation of self-discovery:

1. Every person is endowed with a gift and with talents that drive his or her unique identity.

Have you ever noticed that there is something you can do that seems to come easy to you? It comes to you so effortlessly that it frustrates your friends and coworkers. In most cases, you never noticed until someone pointed it out. Perhaps you can remember names or engage people you've never met at such a level that you feel like an old friend. Perhaps you can remember numbers or get an insight into the meaning of something before anyone else. Perhaps you can see how things go together with very little effort or explain how something works even if you never used the item before. Perhaps you can understand someone's feelings without ever having experienced what they have been through. Most people take their unique personal characteristic for granted. It was not something they learned. It was not something they have to think about. Over time in interactions with others and situations, the recognition of the personal character comes to light. In sustained observation, parents begin to notice something different about each child, something unique. Those associated with raising children will often declare they are amazed at how different each child is, even when they came from the same parents.

Don't be surprised any more, for there is a metaphysical, philosophical, and theological truth that demonstrates each person is endowed with a unique, personal characteristic.

Some call these characteristics talents, strengths, styles, or even skills. The world is full of assessments to identify, qualify, and even quantify the depth and strength of personality characteristics as some way to measure what a person should be doing with their life. Some assessments try to predict the odds for success of life and work options. These are even used to match characteristics for the potential of personal relationships.

Over the years, I have come to reformat the focus, and for the sake of this journey of self-discovery, a primary simple truth emerges: Each person has a Gift, a personal characteristic they are endowed with from the moment they came into existence, the moment they were conceived. They were created, so to speak, with this gift that should be the center point of their life's journey. I define it as their D.N.A.; Divine Natural Attribute. It is part of our soul; it is part of who we uniquely are as an individual. Aristotle referred to this in his treatise on psychology, *On the Soul*. Thomas Aquinas, a student of Aristotle's work, went so far as to reference the soul with supernatural gifts. Supernatural, this writer declares, does not reference the soul's ability to do supernatural things, but rather that the soul received a Gift by the Creator. (Thomas Aquinas, *Summa Contra Gentiles* II, 68)

You have a unique Gift; I have a unique Gift and each person you will encounter today has a unique Gift. Don't let your Gift be confused with your strengths or your skill set. Think of multiple talents as the strengths that feed your ability to live your Gift, to share your Gift and to sustain the energy of your Gift when you have run out of your own energy. Skills, on the other hand, are the functionalities you have learned along the way, in a sense to make up for the demand on you to service a job, a task, or relationship where you do not have talents. I will reference the identifiable characteristic of a Gift in Passage Three.

2. Your calling is self-discovered by applying your Gift to the opportunities that come into your path.

Reflect on the above truth for a moment; it flies in the face of all we have been conditioned to believe about life. Think of the times you have read or heard that life is about setting goals, taking risks, staying the course, maintaining a clear focus, and getting what you want. According to this truth, you discover your destiny as you live your life, applying your Gift and your talents to those opportunities that enter your path. Note the quotable saying, "Life is what happens to you while you are busy making other plans" (John Lennon, "Darling Boy," *Double Fantasy*, 1980). In some elementary way, it supports the notion that life is a continual journey of self-discovery, that there is no arrival until life as we know it comes to an end. Until then, are we students daily engaged with what is happening on our path? It would suggest that opportunities are not something we create but rather something that happens to us. Now, this is a challenging belief for most of us who want to believe that we create our own opportunities and believe that we are in control and self-determined.

If you are truly going to discover yourself and the joy of your life; finding good in everything that happens, this is one Truth you must assume is true until it is proven wrong. As a side note, it has not yet been proven on my journey. Note the quote: "It is not what happens to you, but how you respond to what happens that matters" (1st Century, Greek Philosopher, Epictetus, *The Enchiridon* written by Arrian, a student of Epictetus). So "Life begins with your Gift, not your goal!"

3. As one shares their Gift, the capacity for giving grows in proportion.

If a Gift is a part of the soul and given with Divine Intent (when you were created), then one of its characteristics is

16

unlimited capacity. In other words, the more you share your Gift, the more it has capacity to grow. This is something that can actually be realized in our humanness. Because our Gift is part of our D.N.A., it is applied without a lot of work. Our Gift should come easily and bring its own energy to support its application. Each one of us has felt the energy when we apply our Gift, but that's not to say that most of us have come to acknowledge this fact. As you come to know your Gift and apply it, the energy or spirit that comes to its aid will surprise you. This can be caught on recordings of conversations where people are discussing their interests and talents. When they get close to their Gift, the energy of the conversation tends to go up. You say, "That's just excitement; they are speaking of something they enjoy, something they are passionate about," but I say, "Listen again." The Gift and talents do not come from passion or excitement. It is the other way around: the passion, the energy of excitement, is sustainable. It does not come from the thing we are excited about, but what we *bring* to the thing we are excited about. This is why I remind people, "Don't feel bad if you cannot tell me what you are passionate about. It's not because you are not passionate. It is because you don't know your Gift and where you are being called to apply it, your calling!"

4. The purpose of your life is discovered in the application of the Gift.

Now you can follow the path of these Truths from Gift to application and then to purpose. As you identify your Gift and apply that Gift to the opportunities that come your way, you discover purpose. Purpose then leads you to your calling and the call leads you to your vocation or career. The application of Gift is not restricted to any one point of your life; it is for each part of your life. However, there is a warning here: Don't think you can just sit back and wait for purpose to establish itself in your life. You can't see the mountains if you don't make the trip.

Augustine wrote, "The one who created you, will not confirm you without you." You will never get to know your full potential; the realization of the application of your Gift, unless you live your Gift to the fullest. It is about applying what you can do so naturally to every part of your life. Your Gift is energized in action; that's why when you meet a truly joyful person, it is because all engines are getting traction. Simply stated, they are applying their D.N.A. to everything that comes into their life. When tracking the outcomes of applying your Gift to each encounter with a person or situation, you will come to recognize a pattern. This pattern will guide you to the path of making better choices; to seeing where Divine Intent is leading you — your calling!

5. The depth of meaning in life is qualified by the height of purpose in your life.

Meaning, fulfillment, and joy are not goals or objects; they are outcomes of a well-lived life (Gift) that finds purpose, which leads to a confirmed call to make the world a better place. If this is true, then it makes sense that the higher the purpose, the deeper the experience of meaning and fulfillment. Four simple questions can help here as a precursor to a deeper look later: Who are you? What is your Gift? What opportunities are you applying it to? Who is benefiting most from its application? If you are up to taking a few minutes to recollect — to stop and really think about it — ask yourself these four questions and make a note of what you come up with! Tuck this note away as a reference point as it will be useful when we come to the passage that takes these questions to a deeper level.

Who are you?

What is your gift?

What opportunities are you applying it to?

Who is benefiting most from its application?

We all are asked from time to time what we do, and most of us make the mistake of explaining the base line of our functionality, our work. If someone asks what you do, you may respond by saying, "I'm a teacher!" This is what I mean by a base line. Another teacher who has been through the passages of this book might answer, "I prepare kids for life by teaching them the principles of life through mathematics or social studies." The difference in this response does several things: it declares the purpose of the work and identifies their Gift as a part of life. Also, what they are sharing has a higher purpose, which returns a deeper meaning and fulfillment; they are *living* their Gift. In this case, one could refer to teaching as a vocation; not just a job or career. The application of a Gift to their activity turns a job into a vocation! Let's say you ask another person what they do and they respond, "I am a builder," versus, say, "I build communities where caring people get together to make a difference!" The height of the purpose brings a much deeper meaning to life and work.

6. The quality of the object determines the quality of the actions to achieve it.

The quality of the object of your life and work will determine the actions to be taken and also the quality of those actions. This truth is realized in the flow from the previous Truth. Do not the actions change dramatically when you shift from seeking to teach versus seeking to prepare kids for life through teaching? This truth was first stated by Aristotle as *Teleology* and then confirmed by Thomas Aquinas, who went so far as to state, that the object of life is in Divine nature calling us to the actions of virtue. If the object is to live life in faith, hope, and love, the actions of your life will change dramatically in accordance with the object.

The same is true with organizations. Is the cable television company in the cable business or the entertainment business? Is the cell phone company in the phone business or keeping people connected 24/7? Kodak thought they were in the film business rather than in the business of capturing the magic moments of people's lives; people want to be able to remember long after the moments are over. As a result, for all practical purposes, film is gone, and so is Kodak as we remember it. Truths are relevant as *truth* in every application.

I call it the difference between the IS and the DOES: Teaching "is" versus teaching "does"; work "is" versus work "does."

7. Life is not about what you want it to be, but what it is meant to be.

It is a false belief that any one of us in truth determines the outcome of our life. Life bears witness to this time and time again. What you plan for, yearn for, and build for does not materialize; rather life takes its own course. Things happen! Read any of the great novels of all time that mirror the reality of life. Take the novel *War and Peace,* by Leo Tolstoy, as an example. It narrates sixty years of Russian life as families come to terms with events outside of their control. This is specific to war and how they adapted to change, how they were transformed for the good and for the bad, and how some succeeded and some failed. Life is like sailing. The boat (your life), is bobbing in the water. The wind is likened to the uncontrollable events that happen to you and around you. The sails are your effort to take advantage of the wind to sail to a specific destination or a mark. To the sailor, it is not what happens to you, but how you relate to it (set your sails) to take best advantage of what happens (the wind). A *theologist* (my word for a theologian who applies Divine understanding to life), would say that each life has Divine Intent planted in a Gift that, when applied, helps us set our sails. If there is Divine Intent in life — and I suggest this as Truth — then our goal is *not* to determine our life. Rather, we are to engage the opportunities that come into our life so deeply that we come to recognize the path of Divine Intent. Life has possibilities *and* opportunities. Possibilities are situations we personally create so that we are successful, wealthy, and happy. Opportunities, on the other hand, are situations that come to us without our active determination. Opportunities, when effectively engaged using our Gift and talents, will bring us to meaning, fulfillment, and joy. The true understanding of self and the discovery of your fuller potential does not come from creating possibilities but from engaging opportunities. Think for a moment of the possibilities you had self-determined. Compare the results of those versus the opportunities that you did not determine, the outcome of *those* that you effectively engaged with your gift.

8.   Self-discovery is an inside, not an outside job.

Many people make the mistake of running around asking their friends and acquaintances, some they barely know, "What is the meaning of my life? What should I be doing with my life?" People are trying to get an answer of who they are in their life. This approach will add even more confusion and frustration to your journey, but it is a common approach. Who really knows you well enough to give you a qualified answer to these questions? It is like setting up a focus group of friends without any idea of the material facts around which you want confirmation, much less insights. If you use this methodology, I would suggest that you at least come up with some definition of who you think you are and what you think you are called to do with your life before beginning the conversation. Come with some thesis about yourself that you are seeking to confirm.

The great theologian and philosopher Augustine of Hippo said, "Coming to know one self is an inside, not an outside job." To quote him, "Late have I loved you...you were within and I was in the external world and sought you there and in my unlovely state I plunged into those lovely created things which you made. You were with me and I was not with you. The lovely things kept me far from you, though if they did not have their existence in you; they had no existence at all" (Augustine, *Confessions*).

His point is that we are all tempted to look everywhere in the world for the answer to self-worth, meaning, fulfillment, and joy, but in truth, the answer is inside the reality of your Gift and talents.

Augustine went on to say, "No one knows what he himself is made of, except his own spirit within him, yet there is still some part of him which remains hidden even from his own spirit; but you, Lord, know everything about a human being because you have made him...Let me, then confess what I know about myself and confess too what I do not know, because what I know of myself I know only because you shed light on me and what I do not know I shall remain ignorant about until my darkness becomes like bright noon before your face" (Augustine of Hippo, *Confessions*).

Finally, Augustine from the same document said,

> I look forward, not to what lies ahead of me in this life and will surely pass away, but to my eternal goal. I am intent upon this one purpose, not distracted by other aims and with this goal in view I press on, eager for the prize...Then I shall listen to the sound of your praises and gaze at your beauty ever present, never future, never past. But now my years are but sighs. You,

O Lord, are my only solace. You, my Father, are
eternal. But I am divided between time gone
by and time to come and its course is a mystery to me. My thoughts, the intimate life of my
soul, are torn this way and that in the havoc of
change. (Augustine of Hippo, *Confessions*)

9. The amount of tension in life is directly proportional
    to the gap between what one is meant to be and what
    one has become.

How much tension do you experience? Does it come and go? Is
it sometimes almost too hard to bear? Tension is a bodily sign
that calls us to attention. It is a warning signal that something
is out of alignment. We have all experienced tension at some
time in our lives. One of the reasons people experience tension
is that things don't seem to be aligned; things don't seem to be
right; we should be doing something we are not doing, or say
something we are not saying. From my years of experience, I
would suggest that one of the main reasons we experience tension is that there is something we should be doing that we are
not doing. For example, when we have a Gift that we are not
using or sharing, the tension can be the desire of the Gift itself
calling out for help. The Gift wants to be used; we received it
to be used, to be shared.

Our soul, as Aristotle would say, knows there is a gap
between what is and what could be. Our soul knows that our
Gift can be applied at a higher level of purpose. It knows that
we are not doing what we should be doing. So, it's easy to see
that the wider the gap, the more the tension. The gap here is
the distance between what you were meant to be and what you
have become. Many people discover the tension they sense in
their life can be lessened by simply first acknowledging they
have a Gift, even if they don't know what the Gift is or what
they are called to do with it. Numerous people who have read

this work declare that just coming to understand these truths has lessened their tension. Thus, the very nature of the Gift aligned with our talents and opportunities reduces the tension.

10. Joy is a state of being that results from finding good in all that happens.

People confuse happiness and joy. Happiness comes from acquiring objects the world has to offer. Happiness is about winning, earning, and possessing. One wins the race; one buys the house; one has children, and those children get into the college of their choice. One gets the job they worked hard for; one retires from a job they did not like. A child gets a gift for their birthday that they wanted desperately. One finishes their bucket list. All these are things of the world and, for a short period of time, give the receiver some level of euphoria. Oh, but how that euphoria fades quickly with time. It becomes memories of which pictures and plaques are made. Happiness is not a sustainable state of being but rather a point in time. Joy, on the other hand, is a perpetual state of being that does not fade if one comes to realize that good can still come out of both the good and bad of life. The ups and the downs can bring some good that fuels our transformation. Bad things happen to good people, and good people find good in whatever happens, as Rabbi Harold Kushner wrote in his book *When Bad Things Happen to Good People* (1978).

11. One is inspired in reflection but not confirmed without action.

Do all the thinking, planning, and plotting you want; nothing will come of it until you get off the chair and do something. I can't keep count of the times someone comes to me saying, "My plans never work out! Am I planning the wrong things? Am I planning the wrong way?" First, let me say that planning is not about getting things done; it is about being inspired in the possibilities of what can be done. Planning, like reflection, is taking the time to stop to look around, to consider the reality of a situation, and to look inside to the Gift and the talents that are metaphysically present. It is important to reflect on what is worthy of your created nature, what is worthy of your Gift, and what is worthy of the object for which your Gift is to be applied in purpose. Planning is wasted if you don't take action! Great implementation of a lousy plan is better than no implementation of the greatest plan on earth.

It has come to me that reflecting is where one is inspired, then confirmed in action. No action...no confirmation. It is biblical, "Cast your bread upon the water, for you will find it after many days" (Ecclesiastes 1:11). In other words, throw yourself into what comes your way, and you will be confirmed in many days when and where the harvest grows, a reference to the sowing of rice. Note several truths about this statement: (1) As you take action based on your reflective inspiration, you will discover where your efforts are confirmed and where they are not confirmed. This is very important for what I call *pathing*. (2) If you are on the path of what you are called and meant to do, your confirmation will be obvious. As your actions stray from the path, your actions will fail to be confirmed. (3) Confirmation can come in a several ways: You will find more energy. Connections you don't know will offer some level of assistance. Tasks that need to get done will find support; opportunities will materialize and open doors. Unfortunately, many people spend their lives peddling and getting nowhere. The scenery does not change, and they get no energy from what they are doing; they run out of gas, so to speak. You ask, "How do I avoid this situation?" Simply stated, "It all begins with your Gift applied to the opportunities that come your way, bringing the energy of the spirit to your efforts."

12. Those with true patience find the purpose of their life more clearly.

The wise person learns that patience is the key to much of the clarity that comes to your calling, which is like the farmer who cultivates the soil, plants the seed, and then goes to sleep in the Parable of the Seed and the Sower. "The kingdom…is like a man who casts seed upon the soil; he goes to bed at night and gets up by day and the seed sprouts and grows — how, he himself does not know. The soil produces crops by itself; first the blade, then the head, then the mature grain in the head" (Mark 4:26–27). When you have patience, you take the time to let the energy of the gift and the application of that gift come to the opportunities that come your way. This does not mean that you kick back under a tree and sleep. It demands you to check the progress of the crop and it calls for weed pulling. Some plants will not make it; some of your actions will not bring results and demand some course corrections.

As it says in this passage,

> Behold, the sower went out to sow; and as he sowed, some *seeds* fell beside the road and the birds came and ate them up. Others fell on the rocky places, where they did not have much soil; and immediately they sprang up, because they had no depth of soil. But when the sun had risen, they were scorched; and because they had no root, they withered away. Others fell among the thorns and the thorns came up and choked them out. And others fell on the good soil and yielded a crop, some a hundredfold, some sixty and some thirty. (Matthew 13:1–8)

Not all your efforts will fall on rich soil. Much of what you do will fall on deaf ears — hard ground. Some of your efforts will be taken up by others who want the credit for what you have done. With patience and a commitment to staying the path, you will discover the purpose of what you are meant to do. You will come to understand your life purpose and then find a life of meaning, fulfillment, and joy.

So, there you have them; the basic Twelve twelve Truths of becoming your real self. There is no demand that as part of these passages you believe these Truths, but for your benefit, accept them as part of your journey of self-discovery. There are so many wonderfully connected things in this journey, but you must be a big believer. Big believers end up with big understanding and deeper recognition of all that is good in their lives. Big believers recognize more quickly the opportunities that come into their path. Big believers are fueled by connecting with other big believers and uncommon friends. This is not because they have similar backgrounds or a similar Gift but because they have an understanding of the same Truths. These Truths become the foundation of the path of discovery that leads to a life of meaning, purpose, fulfillment, and joy.

PROLOGUE TO
THE PASSAGES

At this point, you should have an understanding of the Twelve twelve Truths of coming to know yourself and what God is calling you to do with your life. Each of us is wonderfully made by the hand of our creator in His image and likeness (Genesis 1:27). We are fearfully and wonderfully made (Psalm 139:14)! Our individuality is evidenced in our DNA, our Divine Natural Attribute. To fully discover God's Gift within you, you must begin to apply your Gift to come to a better understanding of what you were born to do and fulfill your unique path to purpose.

There are ten passages identified on the pages that follow. Each passage brings you to a deeper level of understanding and a transforming effect in a sense of becoming who you were meant to be from the moment you were created.

As we make the journey through the passages, you will encounter uncommon companions. These are individuals who would not normally be in your circle except they too are on the same journey trying to discover their uniqueness and purpose. They are also seeking to discover the fullness of their Gift by applying it to each opportunity that comes to them. It will be important to share with these uncommon companions your continued commitment to discover what God has designed for your life. The Gift has always been within you, but you have not been awakened to its full potential.

Realize what you are doing is a lifelong journey. There is no perfection in the humanness of our reality. It is the journey itself that brings joy, fulfillment, and meaning to life as you progressively come to understand the reality of your Gift.

Thomas J. Winninger

BECOMING YOUR REAL SELF

N o matter what you call it — changing, developing, reinventing, transforming, adapting, renewing, or regenerating — there is something happening to you every day. Every day you encounter people, situations, challenges and opportunities that call you to respond in a way that helps you get to know something about yourself in an even-deeper way. However, this does not mean that it is happening — that you *are* getting to know yourself at a deeper level — but the call is there. Every day and every moment, you are becoming what you are meant to be, or you are becoming something that you are not meant to be.

Over these many years, I have identified three basic categories of work or lifestyles. There are the *stompers*, those who stomp their way through life, as if they are marching to some predetermined destination at all cost to the people and things around them. They have determined what they want in their life: accomplishments, admiration, and possessions (trophies). They want the better things life offers, as they call them, referred to as success, happiness, and wealth. It would be better for them to determine what they want "out of life" not what they want "in life," but at this early stage of our encounter, I am not yet going to be corrective. It is the difference between possessing the world versus leaving the world a better place. I'm not here to argue that one cannot have both, but it is very rare, equating to the camel that cannot pass through the eye of the needle.

Second, there are the *surfers*, people who go through their whole lives at a very superficial level. It is like they brush by life. For them, there is no engagement, no bounce, no tension, and no call to self-discovery. They think that things don't work out for them because they are not meant to be and because they have very low expectations or very little vested in life: they feel it's OK; nothing gained, nothing lost.

Third, there are the *divers*, those uncommon people who come to know their real self at such a level that they recognize the opportunities that come into their path. They deeply engage their opportunities, realizing that there is something special they can offer that the world needs, making it a better place.

So, which are you; are you the stomper? Do you have it all figured out? You went to college to get a financially beneficial career, determined that if anything was going to be, it would be up to you to set your own course. The plaque on your wall says, "If it is going to be, it is up to me!" You have done a great job on the "me" or "I" part of the equation. This means you have secured a good level of career and financial success, or you are making your way there. Your passion or self-determination is a step-by-step plan that is building a foundation of a life full of things.

Are you the one who is a surfer, superficially surfing through, so busy getting things done? I mean, doing things that you think you need to get done, things that are so very important that you work day and night. Do you make your list each day, the list that never seems to get done? Are you prioritizing the things that you or someone else thinks must get done or your world will fall apart? There is no suggestion here that this is wrong or that it does not have its place in daily life, but anything and everything can be done to an extreme. Everything can be done at the expense of not realizing what truly should be done.

Perhaps you are the diver, seeking to go deeper into the meaning of life. Are you seeking to understand yourself, why you are here, and what you can contribute to affect the world in a positive way? Do you sense a void in your life that puts the words of this song written by Burt Bacharach and Hal David, "What's it all about, Alfie?" as your frame of reference? Do you stop to reflect or wish you could spend a little time contemplating the reality of things or at least the things that you encounter? Do you wonder if you are headed in the right direction and when it is done, will your life and efforts have made a significant difference?

No matter which type you think you are, all of us at one time or another end up experiencing the need to be the diver. We feel the need to step back from life and take a good look. Some of us are brought to this point because we haven't found what we thought our life would be, while others think they have found what they thought their life should be, but their life seems meaningless and unfulfilling to them. It is regrettable that even though most people at some time in their adult life feel the need, they don't dive in; even if they do dive in, they don't swim down very far.

There are several reasons they don't take the plunge: They don't find the path to self-discovery; they don't find a guide to assist, a mentor; and they don't find others to dive with them so there is some accountability for becoming. At this moment, you have the making within your reach of all three. You have this document that will help you discover the path and how to stay on the path. You have a guide built within each of these passages, and if that does not work for you, reach out to me. Finally, there are people all around you on the same journey who you can connect with — uncommon companions. Uncommon companions are not together to teach each other, but rather to make each other accountable to stay true to the call of each passage. You may come from entirely different backgrounds, but you have a common goal.

So, let me ask the questions again: "What are you becoming?" You ask, "How do you know that?" I know this because there are Truths to human existence that have existed since the world came into being. The greatest minds of all times have acknowledged the existence of these Truths. They have tried, sometimes in vain, to put the Truth into language so that the feeble mind, the human creature, could relate them to their life.

Truth is like the DNA of human existence. It is there and has been there from the very beginning. Cultures and people have termed it differently, but its authority is still the same. There have been seasons of times and cultures that have called it the gods, or God, Divine Providence, Mother Nature, the Gospel, the Word, metaphysics, universals, or reality. Without getting into it too deeply at this point, we must acknowledge the confirmation of its existence to Aristotle, Plato, Thomas Aquinas, and Augustine. These icons held that truth is not relative no matter what we say; today it is not your truth and my truth. We cannot hold a single truth to be different. In other words, it cannot be relative to you, what you want it to be, and at the same time relative to me, what I want it to be. Today we call this failure of truth to be *relativism*, which holds that there is no absolute truth. For example, the idea that something can be both true and false at the same time or it can be good and bad or right and wrong. The reason I take time to point this out is that there are basic important Truths to the journey we are entering together, and I will rely on the greatest minds of all time to build the foundation for this work.

As for becoming, Aristotle taught that at every moment you and I are the full unrealized potential of what we will

ever be. This means that life is not about becoming someone else; it is about becoming our real selves. If this is truth, and truth proves its authority over time, then we do not change but rather transform into our metaphysical self—that is, our real self. We are like the caterpillar: it does not change into a butterfly; it is the full potential of a butterfly but takes time to cocoon into what it was meant to be. The butterfly's reality is in the DNA of the caterpillar. For the sake of this work, I have developed a language unique to this work that I will unpack as we move forward. For example, just as Aristotle declared and Thomas Aquinas confirmed, the human character has a soul. So, I say then, that the human character has Divine Natural Attribute (D.N.A.). These are attributes that come into our existence when we are conceived and are with us throughout our life.

The foundational truth of existence is that each of us was endowed from the moment we came into existence with a Gift. The Gift is the seed of our existence; it is an ability, the key ingredient to how we engage everything and everyone in our lives. It is like the yeast that makes bread rise. However, like yeast, it must be recognized and activated. Yeast, when applied in the right way with the dough, gives the dough shape and fullness. Your Gift must be recognized and applied; in this application, each of us realizes the uniqueness of our existence. The Gift is not a skill; it is not a strength; it is not a talent. For the sake of this work, it is a singular ability; a singular character that, when applied in all of your life, acknowledges a connectivity, a path or pattern, a direction that sequentially unfolds before us. I like to call it a convergence of events, people, and opportunities that stack on top of each other. Similarly, when one climbs higher, one can gain a more panoramic view of things.

Life based on Gift, supported by talents, and fueled by the energy of grace, brings the passion of purpose, meaning, fulfillment, and joy to life. It is a life that lands up rather than always stepping down. With our Gift properly applied, a life

becomes a path of upward mobility. This is not a life of pro-
motions or acquisitions (acquiring those things that offer no
lasting gratification); it is a life of more self-identification by
the application of our Gift and talents to Divine Intent. In a
simple way, we are not what we eat; we are our Gift. You are
,at this moment, the fully unrealized potential of what you will
ever be. All your potential is in the Gift and its application. It
is all in the seed that is planted, watered, enlivened by the sun,
air, and nutrition that comes from the soil. Suddenly there is a
transformation; the potential in the seed starts to germinate. It
starts to become what it was meant to be. Our Gift is not something we learn; it is something we do without learning, like the
bumblebee doesn't need to learn to fly. If its mother tried to
teach the pattern of flight, this little creature would probably
respond, "But mom, my wings are too small to carry my body
through the air!" In the 1930s, French entomologist August
Magnan, noted that the insect's flight is impossible; just don't
tell the bumblebee. A biologist, Michael Dickinson, later put
to rest that the wings don't actually move up and down but
rather sideways, similar to a helicopter, making flight possible.
This does not explain the lack of aerodynamics. The Gift is not
its wings, but rather how it applies them in a singular unique
way to elevate the oversized body, allowing it to fulfill its life
purpose of pollination.

So, you ask, "What is my Gift? How can I discover it?
How will it lead me to self-discovery? How will it lead me
to my purpose in life? How does my calling come out of all
this? Why have I never heard this before?" Hold on, you are
way ahead of where you really are! For some, the answers to
these questions take a lifetime. For others, it takes more than
a lifetime, which means they don't get to it in *this* lifetime. Yet,
to a very few, the answers come in a short painful period of
time. You see, to these few, the awakening comes because they
have experienced failure on the path they chose for themselves.
They have lost someone or a relationship because they were

too busy making their life what they wanted it to be rather than coming to acknowledge what their life was meant to be. It can be a wakeup call to get "knocked off your horse," so to speak, by something you did not see coming. Many say that you should "pick yourself up and get back on that horse," but I would suggest that self-discovery or recovery, does not come from getting back on that horse. It is about getting to know yourself before you decide if you are meant to be riding that horse in the first place.

Discovering which horse you were meant to ride does not come to the surfer or the stomper as identified earlier; it comes to the diver. The diver is the one who gets to know themselves before they take riding lessons. The surfer and stomper mistakenly think that learning how to ride will teach them who they are and what they should be doing, only to discover that over time, they will be knocked off a number of horses. Riding does not make you who you are. What you do is not who you are; who you are *should lead* you to what you do. It is the old illustration of the fruit of the tree (Matthew 7:16). The apple tree does not bear prunes naturally; it is an apple tree! Trying to produce a prune because the prune tree does will only result in meaningless effort if you are, in Truth, an apple tree. Just like a tree will be known by its fruit, so a Gift will be known by what it produces. If given the freedom to follow the will of Divine Intent, the purpose will flow. As you apply your Gift to what comes into your path, the opportunities that come to you will not only progressively help you discover your Gift, you will discover the calling for your Gift. The tragic mistake most people make is to squander their Gift on possessing earthly things; as I say, they broker their Gift to acquire the things that they think are important rather than the things that come from Divine Intent.

At this very moment, you are being called to pause and think about what Gift you have been given. What is that one thing that comes naturally to you? What is that one natural ability that comes to you without thinking about it? What can you do that you did not learn to do? What can you do that brings you energy? What is it that you do that you cannot teach others to do?

ARE YOU READY?

L ife's journey is self-discovered by applying your Gift to the opportunities that come into your path. Be advised that none of us are called to change, but rather we are called to transform. We are called to become what we are meant to be. We are called to transform into the original person we were created to be. Are you ready?

Readiness to transform is about receptivity; it is an openness to reality and the willingness to surrender to what comes into the *path.* Most people make the mistake of seeking to change. They seek to transform, and they put on an air of self-determination. We often hear people quote the old maxim, "If it is going to be, it is up to me!" However in reality, most of us have discovered that while we are trying to make it be *up to me,* it takes a turn in a direction that is unexpected. For the sake of your journey of self-discovery, I would suggest that opening yourself to engage with your Gift and talents with what comes to you will bring you to a more meaningful, fulfilling and joyful life.

So, perhaps this is the real, true statement: "If what has come to me is meant to be, it *is* up to me!" To unpack this more fully, we are called to transform, to become by surrendering to and engaging with the opportunities that come into our path.

You will already note that this is one of the most difficult of all the passages in self-discovery. The human condition can view surrender as giving up, giving in, and having to submit to another. This is counter to everything we are taught and everything we experience. I would suggest that *surrender* means to open yourself to people, situations, challenges, and truths. When opening yourself to the opportunities that come our way, we find deeper connections and deeper understanding of how things relate.

There are many reasons why a person's journey to self-discovery ends so early. In this, only the second of the twelve passages, they are already stalled and fail to move forward. If this passage depends on our ability to surrender, and surrender demands a level of trust of situations outside our control, you can see the primary reason we get bogged down right here. "Trust?" you question, "How can I trust; who is trustworthy? How do I know if I can trust someone?" The answer is, you don't know until you do. You will never know who and what you can trust until you trust. It is something that can only become a reality if actions are put in to practice. "Jump, I will catch you!" your fifth-grade classmate said to you, but he didn't catch you, and the bruise you received became a reminder for the rest of your life. Test before you trust. Actually, that is the suggestion of this work: test your trust. You don't have to jump in over your head. For now, just put your foot in the water.

Readiness has a depth of reality. Some people open themselves to change and transformation because something happened that got their attention or because nothing happened at all that got their attention. In my own case, it was not that I was knocked off my horse. It was not because of some tragedy or dramatic course correction; I did not lose a loved one or my job. The point is that you could be reading this book for any number of reasons. We all come to the point of realizing that there is something missing in our life.

I confirm that my epiphany came on October 23rd, in the year 2001, early in the morning, as I am an early riser. You know, I just don't want to miss anything! I'm trying to be funny here. I learned early in my speaking career that preparation is 80 percent of the effectiveness on the platform, and only 20 percent is equated to what you do when you get up there. On this morning, I was prepared. I understood the needs of the group, their challenges and anxieties. For some reason, as I sat on the end of the bed in my hotel room putting my shoes on, I broke down; I mean, I literally started to cry. This caught me off guard, *so* off guard that it took all the energy and interest out of my commitment. I did not want to go down to that ballroom to speak to another group.

For the sake of support information, by this time in my life, I had attained almost everything I had set my heart on. I completed my bucket list. My goal was to be free at fifty-three and from a self-determined standpoint that was true. I had the family, the lifestyle, the travel, the extras and the plaques of appreciation on the wall for numerous activities of service. At that moment, however, I realized that even though I had everything that I once thought was everything, I had nothing. I had success, but I did not have meaning. I had happiness, but it was without joy. I had a busy schedule, but it did not offer fulfillment. At that moment, I felt like St. Paul when Divine Intervention knocked him down. I was blinded by the lack of truth in my life. (Acts 9:3–4) It was so disconcerting that I then committed my work to discovering how I ended up in such a predicament and where I would go from there to regain the reality of my true self. You see, this was the moment it came to me; I had spent my life and career trying to be equivalent to the successful people I had encountered.

At what point will you have your epiphany? Have you been successful, but don't feel fulfilled? You have not reached your expected level of success and don't know why? Maybe it is not an epiphany; it could be a growing understanding that there is much more to your life and you are missing it. There could be numerous reasons, but the most important thing is that you are here. The real question is, "Are you ready to be deeply transformed?" You say, "Yes I am!" But, are you really?

What would indicate that you are not ready? What could be standing in the way of your progress in realizing your fuller potential? What could be your stall points or point? The question is not how much you desire to change, but rather how willing you are to accept freely the opportunities that come to you rather than continuing to determine what you want at all cost of your work and life. One can win the world, but lose the value of your life.

Truth: Readiness is not about creating, searching, determining, developing, or planning; it is about cooperating with what is already coming your way. It is about opening your heart; not your head.

You see, the head tries to make an analytical process of self-discovery. It puts numerical value to attitudes, situational responses and environmental possibilities. It weighs in on the side of assessments of personal characteristics. This author does not argue with strength assessments; it is valid to look as strengths as they feed your Gift applications. However, to say that strengths are the Gift without the readiness to apply them in application and trust the journey to confirmation, will cause failure. If the only objective is to understand styles and how to adjust to them to be effective in work, life and relationships, there will be no real self-discovery.

Readiness is the pattern of surrender; it is an emptying of oneself to be open to where you are being lead.

QUALIFIED READINESS VS. UNQUALIFIED READINESS
What is standing in your way?

Qualified readiness limits the path to the progressive realization of your fuller potential. It is the if/then human approach to life. It is a selective condition that says, "If this happens, then I will do that! If I get the promotion I want, then I will totally commit my energy." Those who barter their Gift like this rarely get the job they want and therefore never know what it means to be fully committed to anything. They don't know how to be passionate and fully engaged in something bigger than themselves. Many people admit they have never discovered their life purpose, never got the job they wanted, or never ended up with the relationships they desired. How could they? They limited what they had to offer until just the right opportunity came along. The individuals that realize their full potential are those who apply their Gift to each opportunity that comes their way. It is those individuals who are constantly preparing themselves, stretching their wings so to speak, whose stars align, or, as I believe, who realize the full benefit of Divine Intent for their life.

Unqualified readiness brings an unlimited path to the progressive realization of your fuller potential. There is no, "If this happens, then I will do this." The person with unqualified readiness is preparing to engage the opportunities ahead by engaging the little opportunities that come with each moment of each day. For them, it is not, should I do this or should I do that? It is, "How can I help you with what I can do best?" I will never forget the quote: *"The more one engages more, the more one receives to engage."* The unqualified ready person: 1) Senses that there is something bigger than themselves at play in their daily life. They embrace the notion that there is Divine Intent or Divine Intervention at work in their willingness to engage. 2) They are coming each day to discover more about their Gift through its application to different opportunities. 3) They are realizing that they experience an energy that comes from the Spirit inside of them when applying their Gift. This energy combines with their energy to help them accomplish things they could not accomplish solely by themselves. 4) At the end of each day, they can identify at least one experience when they shared their Gift to make their world a better place. 5) The person with unqualified readiness realizes a growing fullness of life that comes from sharing their time, talents, and Gift, without reservation.

Max was always waiting for the big break, those fifteen minutes of fame that would launch him into a dream career and an adored life. He had a great gift to gather people together with talents that fed his Gift but was very selective about where he applied his Gift. Max never realized his big chance and spent the rest of his life blaming everyone and everything for his failure. Sadly, many great opportunities came his way, but he was too busy judging the value of each one and therefore missed the real opportunities that had come.

Jessica, on the other hand, was full of life. She found so much energy by just sharing her Gift everywhere she could without reservation. It was not that she received more opportunities than other people, but she could engage more opportunities because she was open. Each time she applied her Gift, she was transforming herself to respond to the next bigger opportunity. She went on to rally others to find their Gift of bringing light to the world.

TRUTH: REAL REAL READINESS SUSTAINS READINESS.

The person that aligns oneself with Truth is the one who will always be the great student. A student who sets a pattern of learning and discovery will always come across insights that others do not uncover. Be a lifelong student; get into things. Get to know the *ins* and *outs* of things that are connected to your life and work. For example, do you just engage in the basics of your job, that is, only the functions that are connected to your job? Instead, get to know the trends that lead your job— the sector in which you work and the world about you. It is the same in relationships. Those that last are the ones where each person seeks to get to know the other at a deeper level.

As life cycles, the relationship offers additional opportunities to learn and discover.

Truth: as you share and apply your Gift, the capacity of your Gift grows in proportion to the sharing.

ROADBLOCKS TO READINESS

Just as transformation is a lifelong journey, readiness takes time over time. Readiness is a deeper pattern of ebb and flow. It is not a steady angle. Even in traumatic circumstances, the shock of a loss or change in environment does not make one immediately ready to transform. In some cases, it may take years to get to a point where the outcome will be a value of knowing oneself well that one can share their unique Gift and talents for the needs of others and situations at a purposeful level that makes a difference in the world.

There is a beginning point, a launch pad moment, when the desire for realizing your full potential is deep enough to begin the journey. Are you at that point? Have you had something happen that stalls you at such a deep level that you cannot launch yourself to learn what you do not know about yourself and what you are called to do with your life? Transformation is recovery from the world and what it offers, which wants to create a dependency that nullifies human determination — your determination.

My work has identified seven roadblocks to readiness. Each roadblock affects people in different ways and at different levels of control.

ROADBLOCK ONE: SUCCESS

It is hard to believe that success would be a roadblock to transformation, but it is one of the most common. Success, the accumulation of all the things the world offers, does not open us to becoming better examples of ourselves. On the other hand, it makes us possessive, dependent on and protective of what we have acquired. Psychologists tell us the more we have, the less we are open to the opportunities that come our way. What we have acquired does not open us to discovering *who* we are. There is a false gratification in having things even if one has worked hard to attain them. As it says in Matthew 5:3, "Blessed are the poor in spirit, for theirs is the kingdom of heaven!"

There is a misconception of success regarding material things: Well-being depends on acquiring all one desires. One cannot be a whole person until one has what is missing in their life. Once one has it all, one will never lack anything again.

ROADBLOCK TWO: LIVING IN THE PAST

Any tendency to live in the failure or accomplishments of the past limits the progressive realization of your fuller potential. There is nothing wrong with learning from the experiences of your life, but to anchor your focus in what has gone before causes false gratification or regret. There is no forward expectation, no forward movement that discloses opportunities. If the past was so much better than the present, then one wants to relive where they came from. Throw out an anchor, imbed it deeply in the bottom of the lake, and then spend the rest of your life floating around it looking at the same scenery. The point is, hoist up the anchor. At least you will float into new waters with new challenges and opportunities. C. S. Lewis was quoted as asking: "Has this world been so kind to you that you should leave it with regret? There are better things ahead than anything we leave behind."

ROADBLOCK THREE: BUSYNESS

You are too busy to have time to get to know your real self! Your day is just too full of things to do; tasks to complete. Even if you prioritize the list based on level 1: absolutes; level 2:

necessaries; or level 3: miscellaneous, you will still have in any day more to do than you can accomplish. There is a social truth that says, "The more time and space you give to nothings, the more nothings you will have on your plate." More appropriately, stated as Parkinson's Law, "Work expands to fill the time available for its completion." (Cyril Parkinson, *The Economist*, 1955) This statement may be the reason that the audience for this book could be under thirty-two and over fifty years of age. Between these years, people are too busy working on the things they think are necessary to sense that there is something they are missing, something that will make a difference in the meaning, joy, and fulfillment of their lives.

ROADBLOCK FOUR: SKEPTICISM

Each of us has a heart and mind with characteristic of references of the right and left side of the brain. The head, or the left side of the brain, wants quantitative reasoning that is factual on which to base its decisions. The heart, or the right side of the brain, wants qualitative reasons upon which to base its intentions. They are as Karol Wojtyla (Pope John Paul II, *Fides et Ratio*, 1993) wrote, "Faith and Reason are like the two wings of the dove." Faith and hope are qualifiable, while reason is quantifiable. Reason is the skeptic's excuse for failure to discover the Divine part of the human spirit. The quantifiable person deals with numbers, data, measurements, length, volume, speed, cost and scientific probability. The qualitative person deals in descriptions, observations, colors, textures, perceptions and Divine Providence.

ROADBLOCK FIVE: PROGRESS BY PERCENTAGES

The progress of self-discovery cannot be determined by percentages. How much more do you know about yourself this year than last year at this same time? Are you 10 percent more knowing? Are you 7 percent more effective? Any percentage is a human limitation on your full unrealized potential. This is equivalent to organizations that want to do 7 percent better than last year. Who picked the 7 percent? It is a dart trying to hit a moving target. Take the lid off your jar and let your Gift and talents, when applied to the opportunities that come into your path be the determining factor of your progress.

ROADBLOCK SIX: HEALTH

Health or physical abilities have nothing to do with readiness. It is the ploy of fitness fanatics that want to attract you to the notion that your physical presence or your health can be a determining factor in finding meaning, fulfillment, and joy. Some would say that the people with the best attitudes are not the skinny, healthy people, but those with health challenges and physical limitations. Health does not bring you joy, meaning, or purpose; it is usually the other way around. It is often in our lack that we find our purpose. In understanding pain, we come to acknowledge the things in our life that are of true value.

ROADBLOCK SEVEN: ARRIVAL

There are two conditions this roadblock refers to: The first is the notion that one has arrived and everything from that time on is a step down. The second is the notion that one needs to arrive to have a meaningful, purposeful, and joyful life. Unfortunately, we set ourselves up for failure by putting arrival points and positions in our life. When we get the bigger house, when I get that promotion, when the kids come along, when the kids graduate, when I retire, or when I receive the top award for my efforts. This is the fallacy of conditioned human mentality that the world loads on our journey.

See, at fifty-three, I had completed my bucket list and had everything I dreamed of, but it was not enough. It never is, but people who don't know any better say, "Then you should have dreamed bigger dreams." Don't give me that bigger dream stuff! It sells a lot of books, but it makes a lot of lives unfulfilled. The truth is, life is not about arrival; it is all about the journey. People take trips like they live their lives. They push to get to the destination, which may or may not live up to their expectations. The true joy is in the planning and what they experience along the way; this should be the bigger part of their travel journal.

Surrender is Not a Weakness

Readiness in its fullness is an act of surrender, not an act of seeking. The wise person said, "Life is what happens to you while you are planning a life that never happens." In a sense, surrender is a prerequisite to readiness. Surrender is a condition of acceptance.

It is not necessary to quantify readiness because your readiness will be discovered in the traction and clarity of your path. However, in this reason-driven society, the human condition does rely on something more tangible than merely feeling or thinking they are ready for the journey to true self-discovery. It is like having clinical trials on philosophy so that one can reason what is truth and at what level of truth the philosophy exists. (I'm trying to make a little humor here for the Aristotelians in the crowd.)

So here it goes…

Your "Readiness Reality Rating": Answer the following questions on the scale of 1–10 with 10 being the closest to where you are at this moment)

1. I am preoccupied with getting things done. (1–10).

2. I am obsessed with setting and achieving my goals. (1–10)

3. I have made a list of things I must accomplish in my life in order to be happy. (1–10)

4. I try to fit too many things in my day. (1–10)

5. I am passionate about checking all the boxes on my to do list. (1–10)

6. I find myself with less energy and joy than in the past. (1–10)

7. I take pride in being self-reliant. (1–10)

8. I have ego driven committments. (1–10)

9. I look to others often to confirm what I should be doing in my life. (1–10)

10. I feel happiness is directly related to my accomplishments. (1–10)

Total your score:

80–100 Probably not ready, (but going through this book will give you a different perspective).

55–79 Somewhat ready (at least feel that what you are doing is not where you should be headed).

36–54 Well on the road (on the way to a deeper level of self-discovery).

10–35 Ready (surrendered to the fact that the future is for you to discover).

"When one is ready, the teacher will appear!" This quote from an unknown author has several meanings, but the one I like the best is, "When one is ready for the journey to discovering your real purpose and full potential, the path comes into focus."

Don't be like those who, when they get older, wish they were younger, for it is not about age; it is true readiness that prepares us to take advantage of all that comes our way. Readiness is the lack of resistance or unencumbered openness. Perhaps being a half-empty glass is truly better than being half full, for half empty indicates a space to be filled; there's room for more.

The lyrics of the Bob Dylan song "My Back Pages" released in 1964 (I was 16) said, "I was much older then, I'm younger than that now." In other words, I am more open now in perspective, even though I am older. You see, it is not necessarily age that makes one ready to discover who they are meant to be.

IDENTIFYING YOUR GIFT

There is so much confusion in this era where everyone seeks some level of self-discovery. Questions like, Who am I? What am I supposed to be doing? What are my strengths? end up in most conversations since the beginning of time. The first personality tests or assessments were introduced in the 1920s. Ever since, there has been a concerted effort to reveal aspects of individual character and psychology. The best known of these assessments are the Myers Briggs Type Indicator and as of late, the Strength Finder. The application of such tools has been applied in relationship and career counseling, employment testing, occupational guidance, and customer interaction management.

The journey is not about finding your strength nor is it about making an inventory to assess where you best fit in the world. This author does not disagree with the intent of the many assessments that are available to direct the participant in how best to relate to themselves, others, or what type of work is most fitted for you. However, the pattern of this study is to identify the natural Gift one possesses, not the strength of styles. Strengths and personality styles can be support for your Gift; however, the strength of skills would be better termed as your talents. The journey of this work is to identify the understanding of what one does naturally, referred to as your Gift, and how that Gift can be applied to opportunities that come our way. This helps us discover the true purpose of our life and our calling. This approach is to note that how the Gift, when applied to opportunities, emerges as purpose and clarifies your call.

The end game is to discover your calling based on your natural Gift and talents. Here we are looking to answer these questions: 1) Who are you? 2) What are you called to do? 3) Who are you called to do it for? 4) What makes you unique?

1. Who are you?

   If you picked out two or three words to describe yourself, what would they be? There are millions to pick from: servant leader, faithful disciple, trusted guide, inspired teacher, innovator, humble helper, field warrior, loving partner, inquisitive researcher, committed friend, loyal patriot, or missionary disciple.

2. What are you doing?

   In twenty-four words or less, describe what you are called to do. For example, inspired teacher! Preparing kids for life by bringing the world into the classroom so they can apply what they learn to real life experiences. "Who are you and what are you doing?" is likened to the reference of the tree and its fruit. "You will know them by their fruits. Grapes are not gathered from thorn bushes or figs from thistles, are they? So, every good tree bears good fruit, but the bad tree bears bad fruit. A good tree cannot produce bad fruit; nor can a bad tree produce good fruit. Every tree that does not bear good fruit is cut down and thrown into the fire. So then, you will know them by their fruits." (Matthew 7:16–20)

3. Who are you called to do it for?

Like most organizations, few people ever consider to whom or for what their Gift is meant to serve. Mistakenly, when asked this question: "Who are you called to serve?" The answer usually is, "Everyone," to which I respond, "You can't be everything to everyone." This misdirected idea has caused organizations to cease doing business ,and individuals become stalled in their path to a meaningful life or call. The intent of each person's Gift or each organization's core competency should be earmarked for a community with the highest need to benefit from it, similar to St. Paul. Although a Jew, he was not called to evangelize the Hebrews, but rather history shows that his ministry was to the Gentiles. His Gift and talents were pathed to bring him directly into contact with those outside Jerusalem. As you journey in self-discovery, the community you are called to serve with your Gift will become evident, just like Paul's; opportunities will come your way to confirm the direction. What is coming your way? What makes you unique?

Uniqueness is never identified in comparison. Uniqueness does not come from what you have that is lacking in others or vice versa. Comparison only leads to judgment and fostering competitive instincts. I have come to believe that leaders do not compete (compare), and competitors never lead. How can anyone be a leader or unique if he or she is always figuring out the differences between themselves and someone else? It is important to realize that your uniqueness is not simply based on the uniqueness of your Gift. There are millions of people with the same Gift. Your uniqueness comes from three things: What Gift have you been given? What opportunities come to you to apply your Gift? What challenges help you focus on the highest need of the opportunities that come your way? These are deeper questions than your personality characteristics or what your strengths are, though these are very relevant. As part of this journey, we position strengths as the energy of support — the skills and talents that support the application of the Gift. Your Gift is that one thing that you do naturally. It is a natural ability to lead, teach, engage, manage, unpack, pack, share, nurture, prepare, and so on. It is hard to get to know yourself if you look at yourself from the outside in. When looking from the outside in, you look at yourself in relationship to things of the world and relationships in that world. If this view is embraced, you will never know anything about yourself beyond the limits of situations, relationships, and environments that you encounter. Your fuller potential cannot be fully realized simply in relationship with current realities.

The mistake in this outside approach is the habit or tendency of asking others who they think you are or what they think you should be doing. The reason we do this is who we are, so why ask ourselves who we are? The mistake in asking others the who and what questions is that they overlay their own aspiration and desires on top of our lost path. This was confirmed again last week by a friend who shared he had asked a friend what he thought he should be doing with his life. The friend answered, "I don't know." My friend inquired further, "Well, what are you passionate about?" His friend responded, "I want answers, not more questions!" He didn't feel he could answer the questions because he has never been passionate about anything. The reason there is so much confusion is that the human condition has it backward. Your path to a life of meaning and fulfillment begins with your Gift, not purpose or passions, not career or job, not meaning nor fulfillment. Purpose, passion, meaning, fulfillment, and satisfaction, come from a Gift applied freely to everything you do.

Consider these simple truths:

1. Purpose comes from the application of Gift.

Since the publication of Rick Warren's wonderful awakening book, *What on Earth Am I Here For?* (2004), the phrase *"a purpose driven life"* has become a household and organizational theme. It has brought a new direction to millions of people regarding how to live at a higher level of calling than just a job or a career. The book has personally meant so much to me in my own journey of personal commitment to live with Divine Intent in my life.

It is very important at this point to confirm that there can be some confusion about beginning with the search for purpose. The call here is to realize that the beginning of finding that purpose is to first seek to identify your unique Gift. We are our Gift; it is what each of us was created with that which identifies our uniqueness and is the foundation of our purpose. Seek first to know your Gift and from that knowledge and you will identify your purpose, "…Each one has received a *special* gift." (1 Peter 4:10) Self-discovery begins with your Gift, then purpose, then passion.

Life flow is created from the Gift, and the more clearly we understand the Gift, the clearer we will understand the purpose that is discovered in the application of it. Application comes with the opportunities that come our way with Divine Intent. I would suggest that life is not driven by purpose; it is driven by the Gift, and when your Gift is applied to our opportunity, it brings us to our purpose and our call.

2. As one applies their Gift in a purposeful way, one is confirmed in your calling.

For example, let's say that because of this reading you begin to realize that what comes to you naturally, your Gift, is *gathering*. For whatever reason, you have a natural inclination to draw others together; you are a gatherer. As you apply the Gift of gathering, people find joy in community with others. As you apply your Gift in different situations or opportunities, the purpose of your Gift is confirmed in a calling. In this case, the calling could be to gather people in their faith to serve God in community. Mrs. Burk discovered her Gift was teaching. From the application of her Gift, she discovered the purpose in her call was to prepare kids for life through faith. Her opportunity was a third-grade classroom for over thirty years.

3. Passion comes from the joy of the call.

Lately, there is a lot of focus on finding the passion in your life. "Where are your passions? Follow your passions! You have to have passion to have a life of meaning and fulfillment!" Don't let these questions and comments make you hard on yourself. As I said previously, "Most of us cannot answer such questions about passion." We think we know what we like, but when one interjects the word passion, there is a lot more pressure. The truth of life's journey in passion is not about things you love or are totally committed to. Passion is the energy that comes from the joy of applying your Gift. Passion then fuels your response. It fuels your commitment to continually take action in applying yourself to your purpose, even when there are roadblocks.

Passion has a unique role in our lives. First, it comes from the joy of doing something that comes naturally to us, and second, it is the energy of the Spirit that fuels us as we face the challenges of staying the course to fulfillment. Passion is what gets us through the roadblocks, the fears, and the reluctance that exists in our human nature. If the purpose you have identified is *not* your true purpose, you will not find passion for it.

4. Meaning or fulfillment is not the object; it is the outcome.

It is very common for people to declare they find no satisfaction, meaning, or fulfillment from what they are doing or what they have done. A young man I met some time ago recently stopped me at the coffee shop to let me know he turned twenty-five yesterday, that his job was going well, but that he has found no satisfaction in it. I reminded him that satisfaction, meaning, and fulfillment are not goals; they are outcomes. They come as a result of our goals or at least the actions that we take to accomplish our goals. More specifically, they come from what you do with all you have been given to share. The higher the purpose for which we use our Gift and talents, the deeper our satisfaction, meaning, and fulfillment will be; these are not quantifiable. There is an inverse relationship between quality of life and quantify of life. In my own experience, the more I focused on the number of speaking engagements, the size of the audience and the number of my readers, the less meaning I found in my work. In the reverse, I found more meaning when I put my focus on the effect my work had on individuals. Mother Teresa is quoted as saying, "Never worry about numbers. Help one person at a time and always start with the person nearest you." With this simple purpose, Mother Teresa founded the Missionaries of Charity, a Catholic religious congregation that in 2012 consisted of over four thousand sisters active in 133 countries. Value will never be established by how many one serves, but by how well one serves *one*.

GIFT VERSUS SKILL

Truth: The key to becoming who you are meant to be is self-understanding and the key to self-understanding is your Gift.

So, what is a Gift and how does one know what is their Gift? There is no analytical answer to these questions. If we accept that a Gift is bigger than our humanness and it is called to be shared, then we come to accept that Gift recognition is the primary journey of self-discovery. Think for a moment: if in truth we are our Gift and our Gift is us, then getting to know our Gift is getting to know ourselves. Most of us are confused because we come to think of ourselves as a package of skills rather than a Gift. This is the main reason that most people never come to know who they are, what they are called to do, or what their fuller potential is. Skills are learned traits that we get so good at we come to believe they make up who we are and what we are called to do. Our Gift, however, is a part of us from the moment we were created and is not learned. Skills come as a result of an activity we seek to get good at doing so we can be productive. It can be as elementary as learning to kick the soccer ball or to program software. There are hundreds of skills that are a part of our life, our work, and even relationships. For example, many of us must learn to engage others in meaningful conversation. Skills are have to's – that is, "I have to learn how to do this if I want to get a good job," or, "I have to learn how to do this if I want to play the game competitively." Think for a moment, just in the past week, of all the skills you have assessed and the skills you think you need to improve. Skills will never be a Gift because they must be learned.

A Gift is not a learned skill; it is a metaphysical character of our nature, our makeup. It is exactly what the word means: It is a Gift, a part of our existence, our being. It is something we do without thinking about it.

We did nothing to get our Gift, and we certainly do not deserve it; it is a freewill trait that came with our created human package. Many people take their Gift for granted, and they take advantage of their Gift selfishly for themselves. It becomes an ego support; the Gift becomes an EGO factor. People who work with people in recovery say the enemy of Gift is EGO, understanding that EGO stands for *edging God out*. If one believes their Gift is from God but then uses it only for personal gain, it is, in fact, edging God out! It is taking advantage of the Gift for selfish reasons. It is brokering the Gift for money, wealth, and fame.

How do we begin to recognize our Gift? At some time in each of our lives we notice that there is something we can do without thinking about it that other people seem to labor over. "How do you do that?" they ask, to which you respond, "How do I do what?" What you do is so unconscious that you don't even recognize what they are referring to. The reverse can also be true. For example, instead of directing someone to do a particular task, (because you know for whatever reason you can do it in a fraction of the time), you just do it yourself. In both cases, one is experiencing the first inkling of a Gift.

There are five characteristics of a Gift: 1) Our Gift is metaphysical, 2) We do it unconsciously. 3) We do it effortlessly. 4) It is unteachable. 5) It is joy filled. To truly be a Gift, these five characteristics must be simultaneously present. These characteristics of a Gift work in collaboration to inspire and confirm.

1. *Metaphysical* means that the Gift is part of our identity; it is part of our nature. It is so natural that it cannot be separated from our persona. People can and will try to take the Gift away by diminishing its value, but it replenishes itself. I say our Gift is in our Divine Naturenature: D.N.A. (Divine Natural Attribute). It came to us when we were created at the moment of conception. BAM! There it was, implanted for life to be discovered and shared, applied in every situation that we encounter.

2. *Unconsciously* applying our Gift is what happens when our Gift is so natural we apply it without thinking; we just do it. In the action of applying it, we notice that something is easier, different, or when another person acknowledges its existence and asks about it.

3. When the Gift brings its own energy, it is *effortless*. It does not deplete our energy resource but multiplies it.

When applying the Gift to situations and people we encounter, we come away energized, ready to go again.

4. The *unteachable* aspect is when we cannot explain how it works. We cannot make it some process or procedure. "Teach me to do that," they ask. We respond, "I don't know; I just do it! You're welcome to work alongside me, but I don't know how to teach you to do it in the same way" (with the same passion).

5. *Joy filled* is the evidence seen; when no matter where we apply our Gift, there is some good that comes from it. This is what I call the Divine Intent of the Gift. "All good giving and every perfect Gift is from above, coming down from the Father of light, with whom there is no alteration or shadow caused by change." (James 1:17) The Gift is bigger than us and is not affected by challenge or change. It is constant, enduring, and continuous if we cooperate by sharing it with others.

On any journey of self-discovery there are roadblocks and challenges; there are temptations and poor choices that can lead us astray. For example, you cannot discover your Gift by focusing on your faults. If you think that approach works, line up with the masses who believe fixing their faults will correct their life's journey. It is the same as thinking you need to study to be better at something that you don't do very well. Now, I am not saying that these are absolute statements, but I have worked with people and organizations who have proven one does not discover your fuller potential by correcting your mistakes or shoring up your weaknesses. I call this leaning backward. Leaning backward only draws you to fall backward. How many times have you heard, "If you could only do such and such, things would get better for you?"

I will continue to declare, "Fixing what does not work will not help you discover what you should be doing. It will make you an expert of fixing things that rarely have any ultimate value." Leaning back is a defensive posture. Leaning forward toward your Gift, toward where your natural energy is coming from, is an offensive posture. Lean into what you do well, and you will find many things will take care of themselves. An offensive posture will always be more valuable than a defensive game. You must move the ball.

Why do most people miss their Gift?

1. They define their identity by their career.

The typical social question is, "What do you do?" or, "Who do you work for?" This is a trap of major proportion. Because of our confusion, we tend to define what we do as who we are. People become their work at the expense of never understanding who they are. We lose our identity in our work. It has become such an epidemic of confusion that people think getting a better job creates a better identity. As a result of this, people come to a point in their life in which their career has been validated, but their life has missed the mark. In reality, life often fails while our work succeeds. Then, there are those who criticize themselves for having a job or career that is less than they think they can be proud of. At this point, the "loser" is tragically reflected in their mirror of life. Thinking that your career makes or breaks you is a fallacy. The truth is, what you do in life makes or breaks you. Focus on the Gift you bring to the work, not the work.

2. They are too busy to notice.

From morning until night, seven days a week, people are busy. They are so busy trying to become something, that they miss being somebody. They live by the relativistic false notion that "The harder I work the more successful I will become."

How many people do you know who go to work early in the morning and drag themselves home at 8:00 or 9:00 P.M. and then fall into bed, drained of whatever it means to be human? Many come to a breaking point either physically or psychologically because of this; they cannot go on, and they just want out. Others make it to retirement thinking things will be better, but is it any better? Certainly, there are exceptions. There is a percentage that finds retirement meaningful and satisfying, but it is not retirement that is meaningful. It is how they apply their Gift that brings meaning.

3. They seek an answer for who they are from the world.

Discovering your Gift is an inside job not and outside task. It is about finding yourself *inside* of you and confirming the answer as you live it in the outside world. The world cannot tell you who you are; it can only confirm what you have discovered about yourself. Job placement assessments, strength finders, and personality inventories only give a first inkling of personality characteristics. They do not go deep enough to disclose who you are. They can inspire you, but only in action can you be confirmed. Augustine in a famous statement said, "God who created you will not save you without *you*." (St Augustine, *Sermo 169*, 13; PL 38,923) In other words, don't be like the farmer who bought the field and stared at it in hope that something would grow. A friend stopped by and asked what he was staring at. His answer was, "I'm watching the plants grow." His friend reminded him that he needed to cultivate the soil, plant the seed, water, and weed if he expected any crop, much less an abundant one. The world will not live your life for you, and it will not tell you who you are without your effort to plant the seed and cultivate the soil.

4. They want to create their own possibilities.

Wanting to be self-made is referred to as relativism; life must be their way for it to be relative to what they want it to be. These are the type of people who clip pictures from magazines of things they believe will make them happy, setting these as goals. For example, they want a boat; they want to be a doctor; they want to be president or married to an attractive person. They want to complete their bucket list. They want, want, want; however, what they really want is control. If what we want does not flow from our Gift and talents, whatever we accomplish will not produce joy, meaning, satisfaction, or fulfillment. In my work, the things we identify for ourselves — the possessions, positions and people — are called possibilities. The things that come to us without our effort I refer to as opportunities. I have discovered that what we choose or try to create for ourselves brings no sustainability; these things do not last and are susceptible to the challenges of time and life. Opportunities, on the other hand, come matched to our Gift and talents. They are part of the Divine Intent for our life. Opportunities are not what we choose; they are things that choose us. Think for a moment of the things that have come to you, things that have come into your path without any effort on your part. Think of it; your life came to you; you did not show up on God's door step and say you wanted to be born.

5. They want to change themselves by changing things.

Jason was in a job he did not like and a career that gave him no satisfaction. He told me it was a dead end, and he was going to quit. He conveyed that if he had the right job, he would be more productive; he would be happier and have a real future. I have heard similar comments from people about relationships. It's not me; it's the person I am in a relationship with. I would say to them, "If you feel that way, go ahead and make a change, but you are taking with you the same old you." After the change in job, an environment, or relationship, you will still have the *same you*. Perhaps that particular job or environment is an opportunity for you to stay and apply yourself in a way of self-discovery. Perhaps it is a call to transform and become the person you were meant to be.

In conclusion, don't let yourself become frustrated with the lack of clarity in discerning your Gift and talents. Life is not about perfection but rather about continuous discovery. There is no arrival in this world, just a continuous journey of self-discovery and a progressive realization of a worthy objective. The other day a twenty-something young adult asked me, "When will I know *exactly* what is my Gift?" I answered, "Never! Take out the word *exactly!* Knowing our Gift is a journey of *continuous* pathing and confirming."

Hint: If you don't know what your Gift is, pretend you know! Identify something that you do without thinking about it, something that brings you energy, something that you can help others with in almost every situation, and then go with it. Write it down; live it; share it; track the confirmation you get from it. Then, your Gift will progressively become clearer!

CONFIRMING YOUR GIFT

R emember at the beginning of this journey I referred to a progressive realization. The upside is, the trip is more important than the arrival when on the journey of becoming what we are meant to be. The arrival is merely a stopping point. Envision yourself as a mountain climber. As you climb, you assess and select the right path. You stretch yourself with each step; grab on to certain rocks that will stabilize your climb; you become stronger as you gain control of the fear. At certain points, you stop to reflect on your progress. This journey is not about the distance to the top or even whether there is a top. It is about the climb; it is about the journey. You can enjoy the view as it changes at each level of the climb. You are reflecting, applying, learning, and surrendering to what the mountain has to offer. In the surrender, you will find your strength.

A friend of mine is a mountaineer. He states that at some point during the climb one is so far into it that there is no going back. When the mountain seems overwhelming is the time to get into the climb. Perhaps what is in front of you has become overwhelming because of not knowing what is to come. This is the time to focus on what is right in front of you—the next step or the next rock to secure a hold.

By now, you have a basic understanding of the Truths of life; you have been exposed to the characteristics and critical importance of Gift identification so you can begin to come to an elementary understanding of personal identity. You should have penciled a few words in a sentence relating what you think your Gift might be.

The key challenge of this passage is to develop a pattern of continuity and continuum. In the years that I have been doing this work, I have never met someone who in an instant says, "This is who I am, and this is what I am meant to do with the rest of my life." I have met numerous people who wish there would be a bolt of lightning moment—an epiphany of self-discovery. They wish to be instantly infused with the answer to their identity so they can just move ahead and live that identity out. Even St. Paul did not know his call when he was knocked down on his way to Damascus. When he came to, he was blind and more confused than ever about his life's mission. His fall was an awakening to the reality that he had missed something in his life journey. It was a Divine Intervention because Paul had missed Divine intention. Like many of us, our failures, falls, and mistakes are an awakening that something bigger than us is about to come into our view. Just like Paul, this is not a point of revelation but a point from which we begin our journey of receiving revelation.

For Paul, it was a call for him to look within himself to discover his Gift and purpose of his life (Acts 9:3-9). History records that even after his sight was restored while with a teacher named Ananias, it was three years of reflection and prayer before Paul even started his journey of discovering a deeper understanding of his purpose. This began the journey of confirmation for the rest of his life, engaging each day with the opportunities that came into his path.

Progressive revelation can be likened to conversion or transformation; it happens over time allowing a deeper level of understanding. We spend our whole lives getting to know the unrealized potential of what we are meant to be. At no point along the way do we suddenly know. Psychologists liken this process to painting a picture that never is totally completed. Each day as we apply what we learn, our Gift is the continuity and continuum of our efforts, the convergence of experiences confirming the discovery of our own reality.

Anyone who takes the time to stop in the middle of their life to do a history analysis quickly sees the events that brought them to where they are at the time of reflection. Out of each experience comes a portion of a path that points to another experience; leading to more of the path. Continuity, continuum, and convergence will bring you to progressively recognize your Gift, your purpose, and your calling by helping you become aware of the value and significance of the opportunities that come your way. This Fourth Passage is about staying focused on the climb or the dive. This passage brings you to an awareness of tuning in to what is all around you from the inside out from the vantage point of your Gift. Divine Intent is always there to provide direction for your Gift on the path; however, we have been given free will to choose to embrace it or stray from it.

The three factors—continuity, continuum, and convergence—show you the flow of your journey or the path. They focus your energy and activity into the direction of self-discovery (Gift) that drives your transformation and your becoming.

Continuity is an unbroken, consistent flow of events that lead you to a deeper understanding of how you got to where you are at this moment. One thing leads to another and another and so on.

Continuum is the process of many parts coming together to support the journey. Each part brings its own unique purpose as it fits with the others to complete what it is meant to be for your life.

Convergence is the moving of these parts toward a union. *Con* means together, while *verge* means toward. In other words, certain things move toward each other.

If we are to truly understand who we are and what we are called to do in our life, we must become aware of the importance of each of these characteristics.

The question at this point is, "What do continuity, continuum and convergence look like in your own life?" Make a list of situations, people, and opportunities that came to you without your effort. Identify those based only on the fact that you were in a certain place at a certain time and then circle the ones which changed the course of your life forever.

After acting in twelve theatrical productions while in high school and summer stock theater, I was accepted into the theater program at Northwestern University. Soon after, I enrolled at Marquette University and was very confused about my future. At MU, I met Marty West, who was a student in broadcast journalism. He invited me to meet the dean of the College of Speech. Four years later, I graduated with a communications degree and landed a job with the *Milwaukee Journal* at WTMJ-TV, an NBC affiliate. I was employed there three years before the job went away. This falling out was followed by a position in the marketing department of a bank holding company where I engaged in writing and speaking to the bank's commercial customers. I decided to leave and try real estate, which offered an opportunity to be a part of a national program called Successful Practice. After real estate, I took the risk of becoming an independent speaker and writer. Over the next thirty-eight years, I was the keynote speaker at over three thousand conferences, published in numerous trade journals, and had written seven books. Needing additional staff, I ran an employment ad; this is when I met my wife. She interviewed with me for the position we were offering; she did not get the job, but we were married six months later which was thirty-seven years ago at the time of this book's development.

As you know, on October 23, 2001, I experienced an epiphany that led me back to school to study philosophy and start this work of self-discovery and finding a life in the midst of work. On and on it has gone until here I am, continuing each day to be humbled by the Truth of life and what each of us is called to become as a result of the appreciation of each one's Gift. I have made many mistakes along the way, thinking I could determine my path and direct my life to the outcomes I wanted for myself. As I look back, even the mistakes were corrective points. They came when I stepped off the path and defused my efforts and, in a sense, squandered my Gift and talents in areas where they did not serve well.

What has your path looked like? What are the key points or events that have led you to where you are at this moment? What has been the flow, the path, the convergence of things positioning your energy? What is the activity that is guiding you toward a direction of transformation?

Continuity, continuum, and convergence are the keys. They are the principles needed to progress so you can truly say that every day and in every way, you are gaining a deeper understanding of who you are and what you are meant to be. I would even propose that falling down can actually be stepping up, and falling back can be progressing forward. My father, Larry Winninger, always said his greatest insight did not come when things were going well. Rather, his greatest insight came when things were not working, when things were not going well. We come to know ourselves in a deeper way while in the midst of failure or loss more than we will ever come to know ourselves in success. So, in truth, each of us must fall to rise; we must fail before we win; we must step down before we land up, for it is in these moments we see our need and have an opportunity to open ourselves to the One who gave us our Gift.

What is getting in the way of your continuity? What is getting in the way of your continuous self-discovery?

71

1. Silo the departments of your life; then seek to find balance in your life.

The mistake the human character continues to make is that it tries to balance life. Each of us, at one time or another, tries to find this elusive objective — life balance. How well are you doing in balancing your life? Life coaches build careers on helping others try to find balance. Books are written on how to quantify it so clearly that you know you are out of balance. My advice is, "Forget it!" Then you ask, "Forget what?" To which I answer, "Forget trying to find balance in your life." You see, you cannot find something that does not exist. Life balance does not exist. This mistaken formula tries to quantify one part of life against another as if they do battle with each other. If you do attain a balanced life, you have attained a divided life. No one can be happy with a divided life, as each part of life is being lived at the expense of another part of your life.

Consider the seven habits of life: relationship, work, activity, service, recreation, rest, and faith. There is an exercise that asks you to rate each one of these seven habits on a scale of 1–10 (10 being the highest) referencing to how well you are doing in each area. Immediately we set up a proposed win/loss relationship between the areas. For example, one might say their work is doing quite well, but at the expense of their relationships. There can be no win-or-lose matrix. If there is a win/lose matrix, there can be no balance. It is impossible, and this drives tension insinuating things in our life are out of line, out of balance. My work has brought me to believe that one is not seeking balance but rather convergence. Truth calls us not to find balance across areas of life, but *convergence* on a single character. As an example, let's look at our Gift and ask ourselves in each of the seven habits, "How well am I applying my Gift?" This is not how *evenly* you are applying your Gift. If your Gift is one of insight, how well are you applying or sharing your insight with those who enter your path?

Faith-filled people, of which I am one, ask me where faith fits into these habits. My response to them is, "If you believe your Gift is Divinely infused at the moment you were created and is from God, then it is part of your faith. If this is your belief, then also believe that anywhere you apply your Gift and faith, you will find a vocation." The word *vocation* in Latin means *call*. Simply stated, as you apply your Gift, you are applying your faith to each part of your life; there is convergence. In doing so, you then have a vocation, a call.

2. Deviate from fit and flow.

Everyone wants to make up their own color pallet to mix and create their painting of their life. Yet, in the scheme of things, certain colors blend well with other colors, like cool colors and warm colors. Now you can put warm and cool colors together and say they are all cool, patting yourself on the back as being creative and feeling liberated. You can try to be anything you think your heart desires, but this does not mean that what you come up with — your personal recipe — will bring you meaning, fulfillment, happiness, and joy. Certain things are meant to go together; they fit like a puzzle. It is the same with the journey of self-discovery. Your Gift and talents lend themselves to fit in a certain way. If you could put on special glasses to see the future or see your life from a fifty-thousand-foot view, this would become apparent. Your set of talents, along with your opportunities, fit together, giving your life flow. Fit and flow are two of the most important truths. It is like a natural law of creation; these work together like the bees with the flower. They work together to complete their part in the lifespan they have been given. Your fit is all about your Gift, and your flow is all about the opportunities that come into your path and how you embrace them. The key is to trust this process so it will be demonstrated to you. Fail to trust it, and you will unconsciously work against it. Trust is critical throughout this journey. Later, we will go into it deeper, as it is about surrender, not relativism or self-determination. It goes against the grain of society's orientation program.

3. Confuse opinion for Truth.

Very little of what each of us hears on a given day is Truth. The majority of all information is opinion disguised as Truth. If you listen carefully you can even hear people allude to some state-ment of Truth. As a broadcast journalism student, I was taught that fact and opinion should be separated for the readers or listener. Today, you can listen to any commentator and hear someone who is trying to convince you that what they are speculating is the Truth. The wonderful aspect of Truth is it has its own authority. Truth is in control, and when given time, will right itself. In other words, if you question whether some-thing is Truth or opinion, be patient. If it is Truth, it will con-firm itself ,and if it is only opinion it will prove itself to not be Truth. When it comes to self-discovery, let the Truth of your Gift confirm itself. Remember, you are inspired in reflection and confirmed in action. If you think you should be doing something, prepare yourself and see if the opportunity shows itself. However, if it does not, be willing to accept the Truth. A few years ago, I sensed a desire to go back to school to get my doctorate in leadership. I was not sure at the time why except that I liked studying and thought it would be another step up in my career and pondered what I could do with a PhD. Well, perhaps I would teach at the university level? Now, that was a question, not a statement, because at that time, I had already lectured at the college level. So, what did I do? I spent hours putting together the extensive application and contacted my old professors from my master's degree days to pester them for letters of recommendation. I went through the interview process to be accepted into the cohort program. What hap-pened? The letter of rejection came. Sorry, you are not what we are looking for. Now I am not saying if or when you receive a rejection letter (that is how most of us take it) that we should not challenge it. If I had surrendered to the rejection with my writing, I would not have published several books. Each road-block is a call to stop and reflect on the question, "What am I doing as a result of this? What am I to learn from this?" It was very insightful when I applied this methodology to my own situation. I realized I had wanted the doctorate for the wrong reason, and because of this, there would be no fulfillment no matter how hard I worked to get it. The meaning is in the purpose for doing it, not the goal of acquiring it.

4. Fail to test for the purpose of Gift.

As I shared in the previous paragraph, are you seeking only to acquire something to fulfill a call to become something that serves yourself? This is the "plaque on the wall" syndrome. In 2001, I built an addition on the house so there would be wall space to display the recognitions I mistakenly felt had confirmed the value of my life. Is the real story about what positions I held; what recognitions I received, or what I have become as a result of what I did in the process of living in the state of service? There is a wonderful acknowledgement in scripture: Psalm 40 reads, "Here I am Lord, I come to do your will." It was the underlying theme of my late father's life. He was very loved and appreciated because his life was one of service. He came to serve using his Gift and talents to help those who came into his life. Whether you believe in the Divine or not, those who ultimately find meaning, purpose, fulfillment, and joy in their life live Psalm 40. I have come to use my Gift and talents to help others, making the world a better place. All lives are called to live a purpose based on the application of their Gift and talents to the highest need of the opportunities that come their way, not the possibilities they seek to create for themselves.

5. Seeking personal gain (does not apply Gift willingly).

During these years, I had acquired several small businesses. Some of them succeeded, and some of them failed. Looking back, I am convinced that the ones I hounded, the ones I went after doggedly, were not meant to succeed. Guess what? They did not succeed! The ones that did work were successful because they were opportunities that had come to us. One opportunity was sold to someone else. It did not work out for that person and *then* the business came to us. The question we must ask ourselves is, "Are we living life and using our Gift and talents solely for personal gain or are we willingly accepting the opportunities and applying what we've been given to what is coming our way?"

The reason so much time was spent identifying these five roadblocks is because they are significant to our continuity, continuum, and convergence. Without these three legs on the stool of life, all our activities become fragmented. Life then has little focus, energy, or flow, and therefore we will continue to search for meaning.

PURPOSE IS DISCOVERED IN THE APPLICATION OF GIFT

Y ou are convinced that great things are going to come to you. You can feel it! They are just around the corner or over the next hill! It will be your big thing; your once-in-a-life-time opportunity. You know it's coming, but it never does, and you can't understand why. You didn't realize that you never got to the corner, nor did you make it to the top of the hill. You were thinking that it would just come to you. This can be the same as people who pray but don't take any action when they are called to take action. They believe if one just has patience and waits, it will land in their lap rather than acting on the call.

When Samuel the prophet was asleep, he heard the Lord's voice, and he rose and ran to Eli. He called out, "Here I am Lord and I come to do your will" (1 Samuel 3:3–10). This passage has always meant a lot to me because I noted that when Samuel heard the Lord's voice he did not lie back and go to sleep. He rose and ran; he took action. He did not continue to lie there hoping that whatever the Lord wanted would come to him without effort.

Many misread the statement I made earlier about opportunities coming your way. It is true they do come your way, but that does not mean you can just idle your life away or stand in the middle of a field and have them fall in your lap. That is not the fuller meaning of the truth of opportunity. Many people say, "I don't need to go to church to find God." That is very true, but being surrounded by God's people and hearing confirmation in Truth helps us recognize God's voice. There is so much confusion in self-discovery. You can find yourself without help; people do. You can even find yourself without God, but you cannot figure out what you are meant to do with your life without the One who created you.

You can find yourself by yourself, but the point of this book is not to just find yourself but rather what you are supposed to do with your life once you do. I will repeat what Augustine said that I noted in the introduction to this book: "The one who created you, will not confirm you without you." Simply stated, that means that you must be in motion; you must interact with the things that come your way. Opportunities come to every one of us, but we don't recognize them as opportunities if we are not in motion, if we are not engaging them in some action. It doesn't even need to be the right action in the right direction; it can be the wrong action or the wrong motion. There is such a fallacy in the statement, "He or she was in the right place at the right time!" If you have opened yourself to the Divine Intent, there is no right time or right place because God is not in time or place; He is all time and all places. The great thing about motion is that we may not necessarily be in motion in the right direction, but we must be open and active. Note the reference here to three words that connote the same thing: action, function, motion. They all refer to "doing something."

We must be doing something to find the path to the purpose of life. That doesn't mean just filling time or always being busy for the sake of keeping oneself busy. Busyness does not have a pathing purpose. Just keeping yourself busy will not result in a clear direction. Often I hear people say, "I was always busy in my life, but I never found meaning." Busy and purpose do not necessarily converge.

Passage five is about the functionality, the application of a Gift. The discovery and deeper understanding of your Gift comes when we use it. In other words, take action by sharing it! As I have stated earlier, remember that your Gift is meant to be shared, not kept to yourself. It makes no difference how deeply you understand your Gift. Taking action or building functionality for its application is the foundation of progressive realization, self-discovery or transformation, whichever you care to call it.

Functionality is more than an action; it is a group of actions or movements that work together for a purpose. For example, the functionality of health is not about exercise or diet; it is a group of activities that work together to support a healthy lifestyle. The functionality of health *could* be described as healthy eating, regular exercise, and plenty of rest. These all work together for a common result. However, society often elevates the end result of simply losing weight as becoming healthy. On the other hand, let's look at prayer as a function of faith. Prayer is not simply about praying. Prayer is about becoming sensitive to the messages of Divine Intent for your life. It is about opening your mind, heart, and soul to the opportunities that are coming to you so you can see the path to your purpose. Prayer is about opening yourself to the truth of character by living the virtues of faith, hope, and charity. This is not just about having faith; it is about living in the truths of life, the Truths of faith. You can argue about the reality of faith or the existence of Divine Intent in your life, but if you do, you may still come to know yourself, but fail to understand what you are called to do with your life. Without some level of faith, hope, and charity (that is, love) you will fail to find deeper purpose. The net result of not finding purpose detours us from finding meaning, fulfillment, and joy.

Functionality, or motion in and of themselves, do not have value if done for the sake of staying busy, but rather its value comes from application. Motion becomes action when you engage opportunities that are being sent your way. These opportunities lead you to the path that leads to the understanding of your Gift and when applied effectively, will bring you to discover your purpose. Do you see the flow? The functionality of Gift when applied to opportunities validates the opportunity and clarifies purpose. Over time, this brings meaning, fulfillment, and joy.

There is a theological truth that states, "We are inspired in reflection, but not confirmed until we take action." We can think about something, mind map the possibilities, and write the proposal and strategic plan, but until we take action, we will never know what the outcome really looks like. How do you know if you are meant to do something if all you do is try to think your way through it? It's like the person who dreams all day but never does anything to make the dream a reality rather than just imaginary.

"You will know them by their fruit!" (Matt. 17:6) Thinking does not produce the fruit. Fruit comes from doing something. Don't just think; act! In taking action, you will prove or disprove the thinking. You will then know the reality of your thinking by the outcome of your actions. If you have a definite belief, your actions should demonstrate what you believe. Actions confirm beliefs, and beliefs are confirmed in actions. If you want to change, you must change your actions (your functions).

Functionality is the key to discovering the reality of your Gift. In a series of related actions, if the outcome is "meant to be" it will be. In the functionality is the confirmation. If you are meant to be an apple tree in the process of producing fruit, you will produce apples, not bananas. The key is to take action and have function; you must go through the process of producing. It's the *IS* and *DOES* of becoming what you are meant to be and do. In each of us exists an IS and a DOES. The tree is the IS and the fruit is the outcome of the DOES. Metaphysically, it is not possible to violate this truth. You can trick the IS into believing that the DOES is different from what it was meant to be, but over time, the false DOES exhaust itself and it becomes virtually impossible to keep up the charade.

During my career of speaking, I was able to propel myself into the Speaker Hall of Fame. I honed the skill of platform speaking, engaging audiences to such a level that they left the conference determined to use the concepts to become a leader I had shared. My interest in the content I was delivering diminished as the years passed, and I came to the realization there was something I was missing. Over time, I realized my true calling and purpose. It was *not* in sharing how to lead by taking command of the situation, but rather in sharing how to lead by getting to know your Gift and talents. It was recognizing that engaging with opportunities will help us understand our purpose. Almost overnight, this realization brought me energy of the spirit and clarity of action. I now had a mission with a feeling of meaning and fulfillment.

Once the *teleos* (the end) or object begins to become clear, the actions to accomplish it begin to appear to confirm the Gift. It is an Aristotelian teaching confirmed by Thomas Aquinas that the defined end draws the actions (functions) to achieve the end. As we have said, "If the right actions do not appear, we should question the validity or clarity of the end or object." For some, this is difficult to embrace. If the object or purpose of your life is true, the opportunities to accomplish it will flow into your path; they will come to you. In performing the actions that engage those opportunities, the object is proved or disproved. In the simplest terms, if you are doing what you are meant to do, what it takes to accomplish it will come to your aid. If the resources are not coming to accomplish your goal, *stop*, pause, and take a good look at the reality of your goal or object. Many will say, "If it is not happening, work harder, get smarter, or do both. Working harder is often working harder on what is not working! How smart is that? You can be a great writer or speaker with the wrong subject matter. There's nothing wrong with being good at what you do; be good at what you were *meant* to be good at. Truly great speakers share what they are meant to share from the insight they discovered by applying their Gift to the opportunities that came to them.

The application of your Gift is the key to finding purpose. In those early years, every time I finished speaking I would come away feeling empty. Something inside of me kept saying, "It's not about the money, it's not about the applause, and it's not about being a popular keynote speaker." After every presentation in each city I would ask, "Then what is it about?" Seemingly, I was using all my training and talents to present the knowledge and depth of a subject to fit the unique need of the group, but something was missing. What was it?

As credible, forceful, and engaging my delivery was from the platform, I came to realize the subject I was presenting was not what I was created to present. It was not the dialogue I was meant to unpack. One day a friend of mine who was also in a speaking career, called me from his home in Florida. He said, "Winninger, you are amazing! I want to be just like you someday. But Thom, you should listen to yourself to discover the reality of yourself. You should listen to your own stuff!" So, thank you, Sam Geist. I did just what you told me to do! I pulled out the box containing the video recordings of my old presentations. As I listened to myself and watched the actions of my presentations, I noticed there were certain moments in my presentation that would seem more natural. Why was that? Why during those moments was it more real? Over and over I listened to those particular moments. It became very clear to me that in those natural and full of energy moments, I was talking about Truth. I was talking about the challenges of real life. At those moments, I was sharing ideas about getting to know your real self and the real purpose of life. It was

fascinating that the more time I spent speaking about Truth and its application, the more fulfillment I felt.

With this in mind, I developed a list of actions that included studying Truth, identifying examples of the alignment of life, and writing about the application of Truth to life and work. It quickly became obvious to me that it can be simply stated: "To be sustainable and relevant, everything must be supported by a truth." Note here that function—the action I took to get to know Truth—confirmed the purpose of my life. Without the function, there is no confirmation. The purpose of my life is to unpack Truth so others like you can realize their purpose by discovering their Gift and the Divine Intent for their life. BAM! When that came together, it pulled everything I was doing into a synergy of convergence. Please realize that this epiphany did not come overnight! It has been over 15 years; every day I call my identifiable purpose into focus so that it is confirmed. Each day I write, blog, interview, guide, produce content, publish, study, and challenge the truth with divergent actions. Each day there are things that work and some that don't work, but with each one there is confirmation to the flow of the path.

If you think you have the Gift of insight and are called to be a teacher preparing children for life, what functions would be part of your journey? Identify the functions where you can apply your Gift. In doing so, you will discover your purpose as it is applied in all the parts of your life and work (YOUR CALL).

The functionality of any Gift includes:

1. Connecting with others who are seeking the answer to questions about self-discovery, the meaning of life, and application of Gift and talents (true DNA).

It is important to develop a group of Uncommon Companions. Associate with people who are drawn together, not because they have similar jobs, talents, or even interests, but rather because they want to know the Divine purpose for their lives. They are together to create some accountability along the journey to self-understanding. Are you doing what you committed to do with each step or passage of the journey? They meet on a regular basis and share their insights and experiences they have had with each of the passages.

2. Build awareness of your Gift and the opportunities that come to you without your own effort.

Awareness and clarity are the keys to transformation. Is your antenna up? Are you tuned into the right channel to start discovering things, people, situations, actions, and personal characteristics that come into your path and have a message or convergence with the real you? Most people fail at discovering themselves because they fail at developing awareness and clarity. Building awareness is about putting together a collage to represent your path, pausing to frame the opportunities in life and taking a step back from them to discover what they are saying to you. Good framing is based on effective questioning. For example, rather than asking the question, "Why did that happen to me?" you would ask, "What am I to learn from that?" or "How does that converge or relate to the other things going on here in the big picture?" Practice focusing your attention on the big picture. Let three images or things in the collage catch your attention. Dwell on the question, "How do these three things relate?" At first, they will not seem to relate, but give it some time. There will be a flow, and a message will begin to form. This same thing takes place in reflective prayer. In reflective prayer, we are opening ourselves to messages related to Divine Intent for our lives. What is our Gift, and what are our talents? What are we meant to do with them in our life? What is the purpose of our efforts? This takes continuous application. It is parallel to moving to a fifty-thousand-foot view of your world and suddenly seeing how the pieces seem to fit together as a map.

3. Develop a sixteen-to-twenty-four word description that describes what you perceive your Gift to be.

Language relates to what you would answer if someone asked you, "What do you do?" I'm not talking about your job but rather the higher purpose of the activity of your life. For much of my life I thought I was a speaker helping businesses grow. Over time through pathing, I came to realize that I was really "unpacking Truth" so that individuals can realize their purpose by discovering their Gift and applying that Gift in the opportunities that came their way, ultimately, identifying their purpose to make the world a better place. Yes, I realize it is more than twenty-four words, but start longer and trim. For example: "Engaging others in discovering their purpose so they realize the fuller potential of Divine Intent."

4. Develop a list of functions (actions) that relate to your Gift.

If your Gift is to engage others in the realization of their own purpose, then what are the functions of your Gift? Remember, a Gift is confirmed in actions. Functions for this Gift could include asking more questions than making statements; ask more open-ended questions than close-ended questions. Use questions that begin with who, what, where, when, how, and why. These are interview questions similar to what a journalist would use. They cannot be answered with a yes, no, or a single-word response. These questions help create conversation. Another function would be to seek out people with life stories that interest you. These are people who have found purpose. It is easier than you think to connect with people. You will often be surprised at the positive response you get from them. Still another function is to write about what you have discovered regarding the interests of others; keep them short as in 250–450 words. Notice that each of these functions are about engaging others, with an interest in others and not an interest in yourself. If your Gift is truly engaging others in the realization of their own purpose, you will have more positive than negative results with these functions. No matter what you think your Gift is, it is imperative to develop actions and functions that support the activity of that Gift. In this, you are seeking confirmation.

5. Adopt a daily routine of morning reflection and evening examination as it relates to the observation you make about your experiences.

Focus yourself at the beginning of each day. Do this by identifying a quest that you will make a part of your day. A daily quest might be, "Lord, help me today to identify when the Spirit is moving within me and around me." As part of the morning reflection, think about what "the energy, movement of the spirit" means to you. Think about how you would recognize this energy or movement. Then, at the end of each day, do an examination of what you have discovered, learned, or observed as a result of your quest. Make a note, "When did I sense the Spirit enlivening me? What was I doing? Who was I with at the time? What was the subject of the conversation?"

6. Develop a habit of the above stated note taking to support your awareness over time of when you have repetitive similar responses from different stimuli.

This does not mean that you need to journal every impulse or insight. Simply make a note of the insights you get during the day. As you come each day to a reflection and examination, you will begin to see convergence. Are there similar answers to different questions and stimuli? Over a period of time, the repetitive nature of your answers will help confirm the path for you in service of Divine Intent. (Google: JesusSpeaking.com)

7. Daily acknowledge from what actions you receive more or less energy or movement.

When we apply our Gift, that which come to us naturally, our efforts will be stimulated by an infusion of energy. In tradition with my faith, I refer to this as the work of the Holy Spirit or Gracegrace. Grace comes to enliven our Gift and make it easier for us to recognize and follow through with the application of our Gift despite the challenges.

As a friend told me at the beginning of this journey, "Prayer is not about sitting and waiting for God to appear and hand you what you are praying for. It is about opening your mind, heart, and soul to the grace that infuses you with the energy and determination to take action in coming to know Him and hear His voice in your life."

You are inspired in reflection (prayer) but confirmed in action! Each of us has a path we were created to walk along. The recognition of what our Gift is and how to apply it leads us to stay on the path (stay the course). When we discover what is not working and detouring us from the right path, we need to focus, listen, and get back on the path. This is wisdom and as Sirach wrote, "Wisdom breathes life into her children…he who loves her, loves life; those who seek her will be embraced by the Lord. He who holds her fast inherits glory…if one trusts her, he will possess her…at first she puts him to the test…fear and dread she brings upon him…then she comes back to bring him happiness" (Sir. 4: 11–19).

TRACTION CONFIRMS THE REALITY OF YOUR GIFT.

A re you getting traction or are you just spinning your wheels? Is the scenery still the same? Are you peddling harder and not getting anywhere? Are your tires connecting with the road, but getting no traction? These are all very relevant questions to the path of self-discovery. If you are following the path to discover what you should be doing with your life, there must be some awareness of a progressive realization, a clearer view of what is happening. Where can you see the confirmation of transformation? Through the previous passages you have come to realize that surrendering to Divine Intent is critical, and you may have identified or at least thought about your Gift. Hopefully you have created several actions that seem to relate to the application of your Gift. Now, as you read Passage Six, it is time to become aware of what is happening around you. It's time to become in tune with the opportunities coming your way. Where is your scenery changing? Where are your actions getting results? Are you moving in the direction that Divine Intent is leading you or are you continuing to pour energy into areas where there are no results?

These are critical observations. We need more than just to feel things are getting clearer or a notion that we're headed in the right direction. We want more than just to continue to assume that if we follow the same path we will eventually discover our Gift and come to know where to apply it to find our life purpose. Feelings are not enough to drive sustainable outcomes and real transformation. Feelings come and go! They are up one day and down the next. Many things and situations can influence our feelings. What we eat, the sun, the rain, our metabolism and the person driving the car behind you in traffic can affect your feelings positively or negatively. Disregard your feelings on the front end. They are no indication that you are any closer to your real self or that you have encountered the Divine Intent in your life until you have totally mastered them. (Not possible in our human condition!)

Joy, for example, is not a feeling, it comes from appreciation. It is an understanding that good can come from everything. Feelings do not fuel transformation or sustain resilience when things don't work out. You may ask someone, "How are you doing today?" Often the answer is one born out of emotions. "I feel good today!" or they might say, "Not so good today. Things just don't seem to be working out." If that person was on the path to self-discovery and the realization of Divine Intent in their life, they would more likely answer, "I have noticed some things about myself that are relevant and that I might want to change," or "I have an opportunity that seems to make sense in terms of my interests and my talents," or "There is an energy coming from some of my actions today that's drawing my interest!"

People might say the latter is what has been called a positive mental attitude. To my understanding, it would be more relevant to say they are on a progressive path of self-realization. They have a pattern of expectation in their spirit. "Wow," you might say, "That is a mouthful!" OK, said simply, "They are living in the moment." They are experiencing life and not just wasting hours and opportunities. They are experiencing traction. Opportunities are coming that confirm they are on the right path and doing the right things. They are aware of positive outcomes to their actions. It is the action-for-action formula. One does something; something happens in response. Notice, I said, "Action begets action." I did not say, "Action begets reaction." If I hit a tennis ball against the wall, when it bounces back is a reaction. It happened as part of my action. It was not an independent responsive action. If I hit the ball to a person and they hit it back to me, this is a convergent independent action. They did not have to hit the ball back. Reactions are not confirmations. I came to realize that awards, standing ovations, and compliments are not confirmations; they are reactions.

There is no energy in a reaction. If a person picks up a piece of luggage for another and the person says thank you, this is a polite reaction; however, it is not a confirmation. If the person who is helped does something to help back, the original act of service now has confirmation. Take this book as an example. If I share it with someone I meet and they send me a thank-you note, this is what I call a reaction. If several days later they tell me how something they read helped them discover their Gift and where they should apply it to make the world a better place, that response is a confirmation. An action for the action is traction! In the second example, you are no longer basing your confirmation on just feelings (reaction) but rather on something that is very tangible.

There are numerous types of traction and someone just agreeing with you is not one of them! Traction can be found in people, places or things. For example:

1. Someone who enters your environment has a need for the benefit of your Gift. An opportunity for the application of your Gift is traction.

2. A situation changes that focuses on your Gift. The focus is traction.

3. A connection appears that confirms your efforts in a certain direction. The connection is traction.

4. You miss something that at first seemed to be an opportunity, but the miss helps you find clarity in another real opportunity. The clarity of the real opportunity brings traction.

We have all heard the axiom that some doors close while at the same time other doors open. The challenge is that rarely does a door close and another happen to open succinctly. There is usually a gap between the timing that challenges our patience. Those who suffer from the human characteristic of impatience mistakenly create a door where there is no door and then kick it open. This causes a life of unhappy choices. The key is to surrender to the doors. I'm not saying, "Don't knock," but when you do knock and it doesn't open, consider that it was the wrong door and perhaps not even a door meant for you. The Word reads, "Knock and it will be open to you!" (Matthew 7:8) This does not mean that any door you decide to knock on will swing open. Note that it says, "It will be open to you! This means the door of Divine Intent will be open to you. It is the door that is meant to be, the door that is meant to be specifically for you. Your door!

There are many successful people who claim they are lucky and doors always open for them. They want you to believe that any door they pick opens for them. Then suddenly the big door, the one they really wanted, does not open as they expected, so they use every ounce of their genius to pry it open far enough to at least shimmy through. When it is their forcefulness rather than it being a part of Divine Intent for their life, they receive no meaning, fulfillment, or joy and don't understand why.

Mark was very lucky. His ducks all lined up, and the things he desired seemed to fall in his lap. He was very gifted, and he used those gifts to get whatever he wanted. To his surprise, the more he attained, the unhappier he became. He found no satisfaction in his prize. You see, he was caught up in the game of life instead of the life of life. He used his Gift not to give but to get. At forty-five he had acquired things most people could only dream of, but he had missed his call; he had missed his real purpose. There was no meaning, fulfillment, or joy.

What went wrong? You see, Mark was driven by acquisition instead of traction. He was not living the moments of his life meant for the journey. He was living for the goalposts instead of the joy of making the world a better place. He was not sharing with others the Gift he had been given, so the game of life ended early, and he found himself alone. The stands were empty, and the lights all turned out. He now had a lot of time in his life yet no life to live for. He didn't understand the reality of life. "God will give you everything you need" (1 Thessalonians 1:2). He missed the Truth that everything in his life was given to him, and he took advantage of everything only for his own benefit.

Traction is the positive affirmation of the application of our Gift to the opportunities that come into each of our lives.

If Mark would have focused on what was coming to him rather than what he was going after, he would not have found himself on the island of self-determination with no satisfaction or fulfillment. He would have discovered that where he ended up was of his own making, not the result of his destiny based on the Divine Intent for his life. Yet even in his loneliness, he tried to gratify himself with the pretense of his mind and the minds of his so-called friends that he had succeeded.

Why do we miss the traction we are naturally getting in applying our Gift?

First, we fail to understand ourselves by competing in a game of win or lose with another person. The human condition tries to find confirmation or traction by comparing what they are accomplishing with what those they emulate have accomplished. Role modeling is a mistaken belief that somehow there is gratification in doing what another is doing and having the need to do it better. Think, for a moment, if it is truth or destiny that we have all been given a unique Gift and placed in a unique set of experiences; how will the comparison produce any real understanding of fuller potential? There is no fuller potential in comparison. Traction is unique to oneself in direct relationship to the Divine Intent for our life.

Second, skepticism is the enemy of confirmation. How can one find any clarity if they don't believe that they can find clarity? Someone recently declared to me in a conversation that they would never find purpose in their life. I responded, "No, you won't find purpose in your life." They then asked, "How do you know that?" I said, "Because you just told me that!" We both laughed, but the reality of this conversation is sad. It is very hard to discover anything or accomplish anything if you don't believe in your heart that you can! The truth is, if you don't believe you can, you won't. Your unconscious self will work in favor of your negative belief.

Third, successive self-observation gets in the way of Divine Intent. Most people are so self-absorbed that the reality of their situation and the clarity of the path for their life becomes obscured. They cannot see the path because everywhere they look they are trying to fit themselves into the landscape; they think the landscape is all about them. The landscape is about others; it is about the environment they are given to affect with their Gift and talents. In other words, the true self does not look for itself, rather it looks for the positive effect it is having on the people and events that come into its path. To understand your potential is not simply looking into a mirror asking. It is about observing the effect your Gift and talents have on those who naturally come into your life. The word says, "Do not let your left hand know what your right hand is doing" (Matt. 6:3). Relishing in your own self-gratification! Quit evaluating each thing you do based on what you will gain as a result of the action you do. Do not give with the expectation that you will receive. Rather, give knowing it is the right thing to do even if you do not receive.

Fourth, the energy of your effort is not enough to sustain your journey of self-discovery. Sustainable energy is the convergence of multiple energies from different sources. None of us arrive alone; none of us accomplish anything worthy of being called an accomplishment totally by ourselves. It has come to light that each of us has a Gift, something that is unique to us. The application of a Gift to people and situations brings a Divine energy of its own that enlivens the physical energy to carry out the application of the Gift. It has also come to light that when a group of people who have different Gifts but the same mission come together, there is an additional enhancement to the accumulated energy. All of us together will accomplish more than any one of us alone.

The key to finding traction in your life, that is, knowing that what you are doing, is leading you to what you should be doing: stay focused and anchored in daily outcomes! Chris Ellis, a noted author on organizational effectiveness, tells us to stay congruent and intentional. At the end of each day, reflect on where during the day the application of your Gift brought a positive result that made a difference. Ask yourself what meaning and fulfillment came from that outcome. As I said, this is not just a question of feeling better, but rather of making a difference. Did you help someone think better of themselves? Did you lead someone to overcome what was standing in their way or demonstrate how good can come from a negative situation? Did you show someone the joy of forgiveness or love someone without a returned expectation?

As you reflect on each of these questions, you will be looking to note something that made a difference or where the outcome was bigger than what you did. The results will be greater than you expect when you reflect in this way. Is there something here that should get your attention? For those of us who believe, we say the hand of God is in the situation and why not? God gave you the Gift! He gave you your life, and he gave you the opportunities to apply your Gift. You were given the Holy Spirit to encourage you to do what you did. Why would God not maximize the outcome of what you did with His help?

Realize that if nothing specific comes into your mind in reflection, it is OK! Also, note that not everything you do on any given day will be confirmed. You will not find traction in everything you do. There could be many days between tractions. This is called *liminal space*, the space between confirmations. As human beings, we all experience periods of void. This may be space between jobs or relationships. Liminal space is not something to run from, but like most people, you will try to get away from it. More mistakes in life are made because people want to get away from liminal space. They think this is the nothingness in the space of existence. However, liminal space is the most valuable time in most of our lives to reflect on what is real! What is your Gift, and what are your talents? What is coming to you that you don't know but should know?

The confirmation of traction comes to those who are not too busy creating activity that leads nowhere. How much of your daily activity is you just trying to keep busy? How much of your day is really the application of your Gift to make the world a better place? Perhaps you are just one of those busy people trying to avoid liminal space. Are you a person who prioritizes what you do based on your own interests or the value of the things that are affected by your work? Prioritize your day based on the value of your object, not your personal interests, and see what happens! Mike decided to change from a person who prioritized his actions based on self-importance to a person whose actions related to the value of what his opportunities were and where his Gift could be applied. He quickly began seeing more fulfillment and meaning in his life. Finally, sourcing the wrong counsel will lead you to miss where your traction is coming from in your daily activity. True counsel is willing to risk telling you something you do not want to hear.

PASSAGE SEVEN
SEEING YOURSELF IN THE REAL

S implicity comes from the convergent application of your Gift to a single purpose. Given the human condition, life, work, and relationships can become complex. In and of itself complexity is not bad, but if left to its own devices, it is the primary cause of life's confusion. Complexity comes when the ever-multiplying objects and choices fail to fit together in a pattern that creates a single flow of satisfactory outcomes. Complexity is a smart phone that offers more stand-alone applications than one would ever use in a lifetime. Complexity is the possession of things for the sake of merely possessing and having things as the primary object of existence. Complexity comes when one person is involved in multiple unconnected activities.

Complexity and clarity cannot exist in the same space. The more complex your life is, the less clarity there is, and the less clarity there is, the more complex your life seems to be. Think of your life as a jigsaw puzzle with over a thousand little pieces, but if the puzzle has no picture to guide you as to how the pieces interconnect, how can you find clarity and understanding? Many people build their career in a fashion of a picture in which some of the pieces find a fit, but because a career is not the wholeness of a life, there are many pieces of the puzzle that never find a fit. In the end, there are pieces of a puzzle on a table that seem to be unusable.

Ned lived a complex life, most things did not work, and he was continually tired and seldom enjoyed relationships or situations. You see, Ned was a pleaser. He wanted to be everything for everyone, and thus, he became nothing for anyone. In each of the situations and people he encountered he would say yes, modify himself, and adapt his personality characteristics. At work, he tried to be confident and energetic, while at home, he tried to be humble and supportive. No one can be both for very long before life comes screeching to a halt. This pleasing approach is like a train trying to go in two directions at the same time. It's easy to see how your life can become very complex. First, in trying to adapt yourself, you lose the real self. As a result of confused character, your identity is not confirmed. You become like a river with no bank, just rising and falling rather than flowing to a certain destination.

When I was growing up my parents gave me a jumbo set of Tinker Toys. There were over one hundred parts including different size wooden spools with holes around the end that sticks could be fit into. An endless list of projects of towers, windmills, trucks, and merry-go-rounds could be made. Even though the projects varied greatly, the parts were always the same; one just needed to creatively fit the parts together in different configurations. As different as the projects were, they all depended on using the same parts. The parts could not be configured into many projects, but the goal was to discover what you could build from the parts you had received. It is the same with life. We each were given certain talents and a Gift, making it possible to do certain things; we are not getting new parts. The journey of life is to take inventory of your parts and discover which projects of life, people and situations come together to be served most effectively. Or, as I like to say,

"Serve at the highest level of need using the Gift you have been given. This is your purpose."

Simplicity brings clarity. It is the unpacking of things until you see the obvious, like the Tinker Toy parts. When you open the package, screw off the lid to the cylinder, and dump them out on the floor; the messy pile of hundreds of parts can be overwhelming. "What will I do with all these pieces?" you ask. Just like life, at times it makes no sense. There are so many pieces that don't seem to fit together. We get scattered and then confused. We try to build a life that does not work, and in doing this, we build relationships that don't work. But the instructions say, "Separate the pieces by category; do an inventory, so to speak." You see, it does not look so messy if it has some level of organization. When you bring certain parts closer to other certain parts that appear to fit together, you begin to see potential.

If we apply this pattern to life, we unpack our characteristics. We identify our Gift and the talents that support that Gift as we discovered in Passage Three. When we connect those parts that seem to fit together, we see a picture of our life forming. This pattern becomes a path, which becomes clearer as we apply our Gift and talents to the opportunities, situations, and people that come our way. The question is not, "What can I build with my parts and my characteristics," but rather the question is, "What am I meant to build; what am I called to build with these parts?"

There are ten reasons people don't find clarity in simplicity:

1. There are those that operate with an "if only" approach. If only I could sing, then I could do this, or if only I were a better speaker I could do that. "If only" personalities experience very complex lives. You are comparing yourself to other people who have different talents and a different Gift than you, but you want to have the same level of achievement. Look closer, as

there are several fallacies operating here. First, no two people have the same call based on the same Gift, and no two people have the same opportunities and life experiences. Second, with different Gifts, no two people can achieve the same outcomes. Note, we are created for different calls with different Gifts, and so as we all come together, the world can find a wholeness. So now you know why the world is not whole and will not be until another time. We as human beings do not come together to fit into the big picture; we don't serve with our unique Gift and talents for the greater purpose.

2. The closets are too full of clutter. The reference to a closet here refers to life. Their lives are too full of stuff. They are too possessive of things, positions, titles, responsibilities, awards, jobs, and relationships. They would state confidently that you can never have too much of a good thing, but that is a fallacy. Too much of many different things only confuses the value of the most important thing. The most important thing is the purpose of your life, which brings everything into clarity and defines the uniqueness of your destiny. For most, the approach needs to be to downsize the list, downsize the items, and downsize the connections. How many people can you know? How many different things can you accomplish? How many different things can you build? Organizations are so guilty of this. When they have done something exceedingly well, they lead themselves to believe they can do everything well! They don't fail in the additional things they approach, but in the process, they fail at the one thing that was done well at the beginning.

3. People lead themselves to believe they need to do what they don't like to do so they can eventually do what they enjoy doing. There is no simplicity in this approach as it builds up tension between "need to do" and "enjoy doing" that is unbearable. This tension consumes the energy that comes from even doing "enjoy doing" things. Their whole focus becomes, "How can I get out of this?" but they never discover how to get out of it. The simple answer is to quit trying to get out of things. Focus on getting into things. Most people who succeed at self-understanding learn more about themselves by attaching to something rather than running from something. In everything that doesn't work there is something that does work. There is also some good that can come from what doesn't seem to work.

4. Lack of direction ignites complexity. If you don't have an idea of who you are and where you can apply your talents and Gift, there are many roads that will lead to dead ends. Any road will lead to you where you don't know you are going. The challenge here is that most people do not pick up on the pattern of their journey, or they will try to travel on several paths at the same time. The paths do not even "converge in the woods," as the poet Robert Frost wrote in his famous work, "The Road Not Taken"! My solution to the secret of confusion in life is not deciding which road, but that many people try to take more than one road. Each road brings different challenges, requiring different Gifts and talents. As one can see, the different challenges and different Gifts create a matrix of complexity that stalls any progressive realization of life's purpose. The only answer to this situation is to just give up the effort to juggle so many things that do not converge and let something emerge on its own. Quit peddling downhill harder

than you are peddling up hill. Coast and see where your bike stops naturally on its own. What is coming your way with less effort?

5. Many will take side roads that are more tempting, but are dead ends. To be honest, this journey to fulfillment, joy, freedom, meaning, and purpose, does require a level of discipline that brings a level of sacrifice. Many want to realize their fuller potential without the actions in their journey. Why sacrifice? Why discipline? They don't realize that the path demands they stay the course. Many, or should I say most, get tempted to go off course by another path that seems more attractive. The world of desire and possessiveness believes in short-term gain at the expense of long-term fulfillment. Every day we are bombarded by messages that encourage us to become possessive of worldly things that will eventually go away. Many assess their personal value by how much of these worldly things they acquire. This type of life becomes very complicated, and when the possessions lose their value as they are guaranteed to do, the individual loses their personal value. The journey to simplicity is about who we are meant to be, not what you are meant to possess.

6. There are those who become compulsively active, taking on everything and anything that fills their daily life with what they perceive as fulfillment. They are so busy coming and going, they don't realize the activity and busyness is leading them to believe they are headed to something bigger. However, they are headed to a wall, and when they hit the wall, it is very difficult to get a perspective on what happened. The need to be busy is a syndrome often referred to as a type A

personality. Besides always being busy, they also think they must be in control of all the activity.

7. There are those who believe that everything is relative to their own situation. It is often referred to as the "Me Mentality." It must always be about them (me). How does it affect me? What does it mean to me? How can it benefit me? They are not concerned with how it fits into the "Us" environment. They see the "need" as isolated from those they encounter. They are the "I don't need to share the road drivers" that make getting anywhere a battle for survival. Honk! Honk! If you are not careful, you will permit them to keep your life on the defense, not the offense. There is no progressive realization of your life's potential if you are always reluctant to step out of your own house.

8. Many get trapped in the reflection syndrome. They become too reflective without acting based on their reflection. They become mind wanderers who are always thinking but never doing. This is the dreamer mentality that never realizes the dream because they never turn the dream into action. It is better to act even if the outcome is not what you expect. Are not positive/negative side effects better than no effect? At least side effects can have a corrective influence on actions that don't turn out as expected. Was the space race about getting a human person on the moon first or was it about all the things that were invented because of the initiative such as cardiac pacemakers, cordless tools, the smoke detector, ear thermometers, improved dental braces, protective paint, and scratch-resistant eye glasses? Side effects give proven value to the action.

9. Divided lives are complex, as each divide (category) of your life, left to its own device, will demand different considerations as action. This group of people think of their work as separate from their relationships. They view work as different from their civic involvement, different from their faith journey, different from their physical health, different from...and so forth. Each part of life becomes a silo unconnected to the other. This creates complication or tension in transitioning from one silo to another. It is, "The now I work, now I recreate, now I parent, now I socialize, now I pray, now I love syndrome." Now how complicated does it get? It gets extremely complicated! My wife calls it the location complication. The grocery store is just too far from where we live. Everything becomes too far to achieve whatever is needed to be perceived as gain. When we moved to Minneapolis she drew an 18-block radius around where our four children would attend school, then identified where we would grocery shop, get haircuts, go to the library, a pharmacy, the convenience store, car service center and park, and so on. She found it all, and for over twenty years our life has been amazing because of it. Now, two of our four adult children have purchased homes within the magic zone. There is always an argument that everything cannot always be convenient, but most factors of life need to fall into the zone. If the purpose of your life and work are not in the magic zone, fulfillment and joy will escape you.

10. Many are drawn to seek the meaning of life from the world. What does the world know that you do not know? The world offers confusing answers to life's most complex questions like, "Why do I exist? What is the meaning of my life? What am supposed to be

doing with my life, and why is my life not working? Why am I not happy or why didn't I get that job? Why doesn't he love me?" You see, the world is confused. How can the world help you get unconfused when it is asking these same questions? Another reason the world cannot help you is because those driving the world have personal interest in getting you to believe their answers. They have put revenue models to their opinions and turned them into coaching, counseling, and consulting careers. I have discovered that the answers to the questions are planted in you and must be nurtured out of you based on your Gift, talents, and opportunities that Divine Intent has planned for you.

There is no stupidity in simplicity. In and of itself, simplicity unpacks complexity to discover the obvious object. For example, when I unpacked my speaking career, it became obvious that engaging others to discover their purpose in life and work was my life mission; this was my destiny. When that happened, my efforts became more convergent, the opportunities became clearer, and the energy of sustainability fueled my efforts.

Take to heart the words of Detrick von Hildebrand, one of the key theologians of last century who wrote, "True simplicity is not a simple thing." And I would add, "But true simplicity has an energy of its own. Once you have discovered the path to understanding you will be drawn to it."

Without trying to read your mind at this point, you are probably thinking, "So how do I simplify my life so I can find clarity in my journey?" And yes, that is the right question at this point in the journey. As a matter of fact, it is the right question at any point in the journey and will continue to be for the rest of your life. Simplicity is a journey, not an arrival.

To stick to the theme of this Passage, we will seek to keep the answer to the question simple. There are two approaches to finding simplicity in daily life:

1. Focus on staying in the moment. Complexity comes when at any moment your mind is busy regretting the past or fearing the future. In other words, you are never in the real moment of life where real things are happening. Living in the moment begins with discipline. Oh darn, discipline — that again. Yes, it is a necessary tool because of our human weakness. The mind must be conditioned to stay in the moment, or at least the day. Just as we seek to live with the understanding of a single Gift, we must seek to understand the answer to a single question. For example, the simple exercise of staying in the moment is to live frequently with the question, "What at this very moment should I be focused on?" Put this on a card! Make this question your screen saver on your computer and smart phone. "What at this very moment should I be focused on?" Repeat after me, "What at this very moment should I be focused on?" You got it, and as a result of this question, you will get it. The repetition of this exercise everyday will bring the action of it from your conscious level to your unconscious level. Gradually you will become like those who naturally stay connected to what is happening around them and to them. This is unlike those who seem to be a deer in the headlights when you encounter them as they are unconnected, regretting the past and fearing the future. How long it takes to turn this conscious action into an unconscious habit is anyone's guess. Dr. Maxwell Maltz, the famous plastic surgeon in the 1960s, estimated that it took his patients twenty-one days to get accustomed to their new look. In 2009, Philippa Lally, a health psychology

researcher at University College London, published a study of ninety-six participants that showed a minimum of sixty-six days, depending on the frequency of repetition, to tune the conscious exercise into an unconscious habit. In actuality, who knows? Start today! Put it in God's hands, and before you know it, you will be spending more time in the present moment benefiting from the simplicity of understanding yourself and what you can offer in every encounter.

2. Make the unity of object the agenda. It sounds complex, but it is fairly simple. This means to live each day with a single theme of your action. For example, my daily theme is to "engage others in discovering their life's purpose." It demands that I encourage each person I meet to have a single purpose for what they are doing. You must have a higher purpose for what you are doing. Your daily theme could be as simple as to look for the good in everything that happens. The importance of this exercise is not in the uniqueness of your daily theme or single purpose of action; rather it is in application of the object in each part of your life. Apply it at work, at home, with social encounters, and during recreational activities. Find good with everyone everywhere. A single theme or object across the breadth of your life will bring depth to your life. You see, most people try to be everything and in everything, with everyone. For your consideration, sample single themes might be: "Be positively excited about everyone you encounter." "Offer up all your challenges and roadblocks for the intention of a better world." "Share the joy of your life with all you encounter." "Be nonjudgmental in all situations." "Encourage others to understand the value of what they do." My father always challenged me to devote my work to something

bigger than myself. Discovering the object of your life begins by identifying the object of a single day.

Simplicity is "The Truth of One": one call, one theme, one gift, one mission, one purpose, and one ultimate object in which everything in your life pivots.

The simple path is like tributaries of a river that flow together to feed the energy of the movement toward the eventual single outlet. The simple life is not one devoid of amazing experiences, people, and opportunities. It is amazing because everything about the experiences, people, and opportunities converge; they fit together. This brings fullness of meaning in a single purpose that you can apply to all aspects and endeavors that come your way with Divine Intent. Too many people wait until the latter time of their life to discover that meaning does not come from how many things you are involved in, but rather in having a central theme in all that you are involved in.

ASKING THE RIGHT QUESTIONS

T he quality of the question determines the quality of the answer. The better the questions you ask about life, character, purpose and mission, the more quality insights will come with the response. Because of my undergraduate studies at Marquette, I had the benefit of several classes in broadcast journalism. It became very evident that good, insightful answers, do not come from poor questions. A real journalist seeks to get to the truth of the situation; they strive to get to the truth and don't pretend to know the truth. They don't try to get people to believe their opinionated statements and pass these statements off as absolute truth. Many people make the same mistake as they pretend they know who they are and seek others to buy into it. When their lives don't work out, they don't understand that their so-called self-truth was not a truth at all; it was not supposed to be their truth in the first place. Today, it is very difficult to separate the facts from the proposed facts, which in reality are just fiction seeking to be fact. When proposed statements turn out to be fiction, no one seems to care about the false source.

The same thing happens on the journey of self-discovery. The ability to ask good questions, listen for the answers, and take the response to contemplation, is critically necessary. Like the fake journalist, the false self develops the answers for the questions of existence and then tries to prove them true. How many times did I tell myself that I was meant to be a speaker and then sought every opportunity to be a great speaker to validate my own answers? This was not the path of true self-discovery. The true path is not based on speculation or actions to prove the speculation to be true. It is rather about asking a good question, contemplating the answer, and then letting the path bring the confirmation. Much of the confusion in my own life was based on *compulsive action orientation*. CAO as I call it, is really initiating many things on different paths with the hope that the thing you are meant to do shows up as what works, making the right path obvious. Not so! This approach just fuels more confusion, exhaustion, and burnout, developing a potential seed bed for a case of deep frustration and lack of energy.

The correct answers come from good questions when the path is meant to be. For example, in my own situation, they came to me when I asked the question, "Where does energy (the Spirit spirit of Divine Intent) come to me?" The answer was obvious. The energy, the joy, and fascination came in the preparation, not the presentation. Spending hours poring over information, unpacking complex situations, and interviewing thought leaders gave me the greatest energy. I find that same energy in the interviewing stage of guiding someone to discover his or her own deeper purpose. That energy of joy comes when I am seeking insights, not when I am presenting. What a wakeup call for me after all these years! The scripture says, "Knock and it shall be open to you." It did not say speak and it shall be open to you. Now this is not to discredit the three thousand–plus speeches I gave to independent business audiences. I liken those speeches to the train that ran on my track of insights. The speeches were the vehicle to get my message to the destination. Somewhere along the journey of life, the object shifted from gaining insights to just giving another speech. A similar outcome would take effect if the focus of a book shifted from the message content to the focus instead being about the cover design or the title. It is not uncommon to have the major effort of a book not be in the depth of the message it brings, but rather the mechanics of producing and marketing the book. Speakers will often erroneously say they need another book, but that is not the truth. What they need is a deeper message that engages the reader or listener in understanding something about themselves that will bring a new perspective in their life.

It has come to my deeper consideration that as human beings with souls, we exist in two dimensions, two spaces; we exit in a secular space and a sacred space. The secular dimension is contained within our human dimension while the sacred dimension is bigger than the dimension and cannot be confined within our humanness. Think of the sacred as your heart and the secular as your mind. The heart has often made better decisions than the mind. Think about secular as reasoning and sacred as contemplating. Reasoning with logic only limits the ability of self-discovery. A linear thinker will identify a direct connected path, but often the path is in the opposite direction of where they think they are being called. Can you imagine making a trip directly from point A to point B, example, from Denver to Flagstaff and missing the Grand Canyon? People who process their self-discovery in this way will end up in a dissatisfying place. Linear flow is from a place, while a path is a flow to a place. Jesus called Matthew to follow him. History reminds us that Matthew was a wealthy tax collector in the eastern Mediterranean at the time of the Roman occupation. Matthew was being called to follow Christ and spread the good news. He was not being called from tax collecting but was being "called to" professing the faith. The philosopher would say, "It is more effective to have a place you are headed toward rather than a place you are coming from." A major question that leads to self-discovery is, What are you being called to rather than what are you being called from? Where is the energy of your daily life coming from to you? What are you being introduced to that excites you?

So, few people ever begin to listen and fewer yet hear something that calls them to the truth of themselves. Think about it. If you don't listen, you will not hear. If you do not hear, you will not engage, and if you don't engage in what you are hearing, you will not take action in the right direction. The rich man, the no-name character in the parable of Lazarus, could not hear Lazarus because he was too full of himself and living his life the way he wanted to live it. (Lk. 16:19) Not only could he not hear Lazarus, he could not really see him or his need. He had built a wall and a gate to block his life from Truth. The no-name rich man ran out of time when he finally listened and ended up in the nether world. He never got the idea that Lazarus was a messenger; he was a wake-up call sent with Divine Intent. What message is Lazarus bringing to you today? What is the Divine Intent for your life? Who is your Lazarus? What or who is your wake-up call? Will it be the loss of a friend, the loss of a job, the failure of a relationship, or the failure of your health? How about the recognition that no matter how successful you have been, there is no feeling of fulfillment?

Be warned: nothing on this journey of self-discovery is immediate; it takes time. Sometimes it takes a long time, and sometimes it can be a lifetime. No matter how long it takes, it is of no difference, as long as you stay on the path to finding the Divine's Intent intent for your life.

Listening effectively demands a level of devotion. The discipline of hearing is based on your commitment to staying the course; it is in the devotion. I define devotion as the commitment to continue to listen even when you don't feel like it, even when you don't think you hear something. Prayer is the beginning. It is the opening of the mind, heart, and soul to hear the language of Divine Intent. Devotion is the energy to stay at prayer so that the walls of resistance melt away and you can hear the message that was already present in your life. Actually, it has been there since the beginning of your life. It came the moment when you were created and then is strengthened with the energy of the Spirit that comes to you along the way.

Listening is the key to hearing what you are being called to do with your life, and hearing is the key outcome from asking great questions. Hearing the call is like conversion. It does not happen in a moment and then you can go back to doing what you were doing before you were awoken. Conversion is a lifetime journey of transformation. Some may feel they are engaging in a backward motion, but it is not that at all. It is about getting in touch with your true self, the person you were created to be. It is a forward motion of identifying your Gift and the application of that Gift as you discover your call. In my personal case, aside from the liturgical rite of Baptism, conversion — the journey to self through the Divine — did not begin from a fall off a horse like Paul on his way to Damascus (which historically might not have been a horse). It was an emptiness so painful that I would double over. At first, I thought it may be appendicitis, but then remembered my appendix had been removed years before. The pain I experienced felt like the fear of jumping out of an airplane without a parachute; the only way is down. Now I haven't jumped out of an airplane either, but the fear of falling has always caught my attention. The statement, "Something is not right in my life," kept coming to me with a backup chorus of, "Nothing is right in your life." I was stunned with the message. I had spent thirty years trying to make everything in my life work. From a physical financial point of view, my life was pretty good. Pain does not come from having everything in your life working, or does it? Pain can come if it is the wrong everything!

In Paul's letter to Timothy he wrote, "The only way to come to know your call is to be sensitive to the needs of others, devoted to the Divine Intent, patient and good." Paul said, "The more we apply these attributes to our daily life, the more we will hear." The more we hear, the more we will understand, and we can become what we are meant to be. Who is the Lazarus in your life? Who or what has caused you to wake up to the journey of self-discovery? Are you allowing transformation?

RECOLLECTION AND CONTEMPLATION

There is no recognition of your life's purpose without contemplation! The train in your brain keeps you from understanding the message of life that is coming your way. I reference a train because this constant movement is like a train that has hundreds of boxcars rushing past with no hope of stopping. So many boxcars — ideas and impressions — come to your mind each moment, making it impossible to get deep enough into any impression or idea to understand its meaning in the scope of your life.

In addition to all the impressions cramming the space of the conscious mind each moment, there is the layer of distraction from the subconscious that is playing games below the surface of your cognitive recognition. Think how hard it is to focus on any one thing long enough to get the meaning of it. All of us have this mental thinking disability in differing degrees. How often do you think, "I can't concentrate! I need to stay focused! There are too many interruptions for me to get anything figured out."

Why do people go on retreat, locking themselves up in places where there is less distraction? How about those who take sabbaticals? All of these are attempts to stop the train—to stop the interruptions of the mental and physical kind. Getting free is finding peace so the purpose of your life can flow into the cognitive space in your mind which allows you to truly ponder the answers to the significant questions of your life. Questions like, Why do I exist and what is the purpose of my life? What am I supposed to be doing with my life? What is my Gift and what talents are being applied to support that Gift? What does the Divine want me to do with my life?

A common mistake is made when we try to concentrate our way into insightful thinking. We mistakenly try to focus in order to find the answers to the biggest unanswered questions of human existence. Some people try mind mapping and prayer, while others will enlist the services of a life coach. In some way, each of these can help, but what I am talking about here is not concentration or focus, rather it is un-concentration, an un-focus. There is a flow that comes from un-attachment. There is a peace that comes when we quit our pondering, focusing and concentrating. I don't know about you, but I get more frustrated and unfocused the harder I try to get focused or concentrate. You see, the answer is really about surrendering. It is about dropping your guard to ideas and impressions. The real insight flows from the reality of what we were created for. It is about letting your outward seeking become the inward flow of awakening. This is not about figuring out what you want to be in your life and then, with full force, going after it. When using the full-force approach, few ever find any meaning, satisfaction, or joy in what they attain. I have heard so many say, "I achieved all of my goals, but never achieved the meaning of my life." We need to let Divine Intent surface in our lives to the point where we understand what we were created to be and the reality of what we are created to do with our life.

There is a tension in our humanness between making it happen and letting it happen. It is the difference between going after something and letting that something come to you, then engaging what is coming with every ounce of your spirit. It is the difference between what you think you want and what Divine Intent wants for you. Take this as truth: Divine Intent wants more for you than you will ever be able to attain for yourself. You ask, "How is that possible? I have big dreams and have accomplished more than anyone I know!" Think about it: your dreams are finite while the Divine plan is infinite. The Divine knows you better than you will ever know yourself. Divine possibilities become your opportunities. Opportunities can become reality before any of your own desires ever find tangibility.

So, you ask, "How do I find this level of self-understanding so I can find the purpose of my life?" It's not about making a list of your desires, turning your desires into actions, and then prioritizing those actions with the most important first. I'm not saying that this process of strategizing your life will not be a part of this path, but it is not where to start. Once you have discovered who you are and what you are supposed to be doing with your life, then you can do all the strategizing you want. However, strategy is action oriented, not insight oriented. The insights come first, then the strategy; first the river and then the well. First, we must reflect, recollect, and contemplate; then we take action to confirm the insights. Remember the truth that states, "We are inspired in reflection and confirmed in action." It is impossible to dream yourself into the new world. You must take action to confirm your insight or correct your insight. In Luke's gospel, we read about Jesus collecting the seventy-two and then sending them off two by two to be confirmed in every town he intended to go. (Lk. 10:1–12) Note: "To be confirmed." If they did not receive a welcome response in the town where he intended to go himself, he said, "Do not stay; leave for a place where you get a positive reception; this is a confirmation."

Practice the pattern of reflection, recollection, and contemplation. Reflection is like getting the train out of the station. It is a stream of consciousness with impressions and ideas that are tied together with no flow, just connected like boxcars. Recollection is a mind-stopping method of catching on to one of the impressions, (ideas) long enough to get on board. Contemplation is the activity of unpacking the impression so deeply that you become aware of its opportunities. It is when you become aware of its connections and the relationship, not only to the environment where you exist, but also to the energy that is fueled by the Spirit, which is connected to your Gift. It is the awakening to how your Gift can be applied to the opportunities that are coming to you. When I first started my speaking career, I was energized by the fact that with a little research, I could formulate a presentation. With my high level of energy and a few skills that I learned in how to outline a keynote presentation, I thought I could speak on almost anything. Management, business growth, and supervisory techniques are just a few of the many topics. After the topic was named, I would then check it out and add a couple of relevant real-life experiences of my own. I learned to tell a good story, list several "take action" points, and present in a relatively engaging format. Now realize, it is not all as easy as that. I actually spent hours preparing the outlines, key ideas, and actions that came from the phone interviews I made prior to the speaking engagement. To that end, I have done over 12,000 interviews in my career. After a few successes on the platform, I quickly became aware that it would never be the breadth of my work, but rather the depth of my work that would be the central core of me. Once the theme of my work came into clarity, the speeches, books, audio tracks, and YouTube videos came. Notice how I said, "came." The river of my life that came through effective reflection, recollection, and contemplation, eventually lead me to the path of Divine Intent for my life. My foundation truth had finally come to light: "We are all created with a Gift that leads us to the purpose of Divine Intent in our life. Over time, the result will be a life full of fulfillment, meaning, and joy." The beauty of this truth is that no matter what your adult age, your job, your education, or your location, you can apply your Gift with purpose to everything that is happening to you, in you, and around you.

Contemplation is not reflection as you're sitting somewhere in the park, a library or in a church aimlessly thinking about a myriad of things that rush into your mind with the hope that something that is rushing through will catch the attention of your desires. The pattern begins with reflection, but does not get stalled there. Reflection becomes recollection that leads to contemplation. Reflection can simply be likened to a river always in motion, aimlessly taking whatever shape the banks of the river take. It never gets very deep and must be damned up to be navigable. Contemplation, on the other hand, is likened to a well that goes deep into the ground. Tim Murray, a friend, reminded me, "Reflection is like a train of boxcars rushing through your brain, quickly passing by with no point of reference, just a lot of fast moving images. It gains no positive outcome until you jump into one of the open boxcars." Grab onto one idea and then ride with the idea, sticking with it to see where the train is headed and where your life is headed without your direct influence. Let the direction be Divine Intent. It is important to note that reflection cannot become contemplation without first recollecting. This is what Tim was referring to by directing us to jump into one of the moving boxcars. Some have referred to recollecting as a process of stopping the train so you can get on, but in my experience the brain train will never stop, at least not in this lifetime. There is no stopping to jump on! There is no easy way to recollection. It is a process of running alongside the idea (boxcar,) as fast as you can, grabbing on to anything that will keep you attached to it, and then jumping into the open door. There will be new scenery along the way, changing the view of the idea (boxcar.) It can be quite a ride, but don't lose focus.

There is a secret to turning recollection into contemplation; it is referred generally to as concentration. It is a mental game fueled by the Spirit that isolates the idea and keeps you focused. When the idea is one you are meant to follow, the Spirit comes and brings energy to that idea. The energy gives you a strength of action. The action, when applied, makes everything better with every encounter. I refer to concentration as closed loop. As you unpack the idea that you are meant to follow, the Spirit helps you hold on. As you hold on to the idea there is a level of understanding. Your contemplation brings focus which leads to a deeper understanding. In the same way, self-discovery is a closed loop process as the energy of the Spirit directed by Divine Intent, leads you to a continuous deeper understanding of your fuller potential. This connection between you, your Gift, your purpose, and calling, becomes more sustainable. This sustainability should not depend on your determination to stay connected, but rather it is fueled by the energy that comes from understanding and applying your Gift to the opportunities that come into your path.

This book began as one of those boxcars. Just look how deep and far it has come since we jumped in together. Riding along from reflection, through recollection, to contemplation, is simply continuing the pattern of asking questions. It is not in people, but the things or ideas themselves. For example, the questions I asked myself at the beginning of this journey: "What will happen as a result of writing this book?" "What will I discover from writing it, and how will it help others?" "What doors will I pass through as my self-discovery progresses?" "How can I most effectively share with others so that the journey will make life more fulfilling for them?" "How can I lead them through the shallow, painful, wanting times of the journey so that they will be buoyed up?" Note, there are no "whys" in this series of questions. You see, the why of the journey comes as a result of the journey itself. It is Divinely divinely disclosed by the Spirit and in opportunities provided to confirm your path.

To apply what you have read in Passage Nine, you must develop a routine of reflection. Stop some place and take some time on a daily basis to reflect. In the reflection, pick out something in your thought pattern that catches your attention. Concentrate on what that thing is and how it relates to you. Ask for insights into the meaning of that thought or thing in your life. Keep a daily journal of thoughts and experiences that converge with the focus. Let's say in your reflection, the concept of joy comes to you. Pause, then contemplate on what joy means to you. When do you have feelings of joy? What energy do you get from doing what you're doing when you feel joy?

THE CONCLUSION: WHERE TO GO FROM HERE

M istakenly, much of my life was about trying to draw straight lines between two points. Think of all you miss if the only thing you focus on is the distance between and not the scenery. When you draw straight lines in your life you miss the fullness of the possibilities that contribute to the depth of understanding. Mathematicians argue that a straight line is the shortest distance between two points, but in truth, this thought process does not consider Divine Intent. There are no straight lines when it comes to the Divine. Per the Divine, all things come to contribute to the value of the journey of purpose and self-discovery. Rather than using a linear thought process as an approach, consider what I call the looping approach. In looping, we embrace so much more! In the looping approach, we can see the opportunities coming our way; we can consider the influence of everything. In the linear, we perceive that which will block the direct path to a destination we have predetermined. The looping approach is more organized. It suggests not isolating your choice of careers, but rather identifying your Gift and talents and then following the opportunities that come your way to bring convergent insight. It is about letting it happen to you rather than making it happen for you. Now, I'm not suggesting to be a boat in a storm that is going to be beaten by the waves. Keep the sail full. Keep the tiller firmly in hand and break into the waves. Don't be tossed by the side motion of the wave; you will eventually see the dawn. Embrace the tide. If you don't fight it, the sunrise will come to show you the proper destination. The linear thinker will set a goal, develop a strategy, and formulate a plan. They will determine costs, activate the plan, measure the progress, and then adjust the plan again, focusing only on the goal of getting there. The looping thinker will look at what is happening in his or her connected environment. He or she will gather relevant information, identify questions to be asked, and interactively share with others. They will recognize a pattern and move with the pattern toward their calling. The looping approach demands patience and surrender to be guided by the opportunities in your path. We must accept confirmation and acknowledge the path it is leading us on. It is about being immersed in something much bigger than ourselves.

In the months that followed in my call to awaken, I decided to step out and apply the looping process to my own situation.

My life was full, but my spirit was empty. I had everything the world had to offer, yet I felt empty of what truly had meaning, purpose, fulfillment, and joy. It became my obsession to ask the most basic, yet unanswered questions of all time, questions like, "Why do I exist? What is the purpose of my life? What am I supposed to do with the rest of my life?" I decided that the spirit part of my life was wanting. "How would my life truly have meaning and how can I make the world a better place using my talents and Gift?"

To this end I searched educational opportunities that would challenge me and would take me to a deeper level of understanding. I needed to understand the why and how of life and how it related to my work. Unlike those who seek to get an MBA to improve their career opportunities, it was my decision to challenge myself to think more conceptually and manage things at a deeper level of value. At the University of St. Thomas, I discovered a master's program that was interdisciplinary in philosophy and theology. It included studies with the likes of Aristotle, Thomas Aquinas, Augustine, De Lubac, Karl Wojtyla (Pope John Paul II), and Dietrich Von Hildebrand. This was a little scary for a kid like me who was not a great student. Studies did not come easy to me, thinking did not come easy to me, and understanding complexity was overwhelming. Something was driving me to find the answers to the "what and why" of my life. Long story short, I applied to the master's program and was rejected. The letter came in the mail: "We regret to inform you that you have not been accepted!" Wow, that knocked me off my horse. By this time, I knew what rejections felt like as I had experienced them in the process of seeking publishers for previous books I had written. "Should I forget it?" I asked myself. "Throw the letter away; you are fifty-three years old! Besides, you are probably not up to the rigors of such a deep program." The pain of my frustration and desire to study at a deeper level began to overtake me. As I look back, I am confirmed that it was the grace of the Holy Spirit driving me to follow Divine Intent in my life that helped me find the strength to stay on the path. I made a call to the dean, who, by the way, was young enough to be one of my children! After entering her office, I began by thanking her for meeting with me. I then jumped right into my frustration, "I don't understand why I was rejected!" "You were not rejected," she said. "Your application and GPA from your undergraduate college did not qualify you for application. Your GPA was not high enough for consideration, and the writing style of your books is not in line with our MLA writing format." My mind was thinking, "My GPA is three decades old and will not meet the high standard of today's smart kids." Again, with the inspiration of the Spirit I asked, "Are there any alternatives to application?" "Yes," she said, "As a matter of fact, there is

one. You can audit two classes, write two papers and get rec-
ommendations from the two professors that you are equal to
the learning level. We will then accept you into the program."
Well, what did I have to lose? I would be learning whether it
qualified for credit or not.

By the time this took place, the only class still open for
the summer semester was Thomistic Moral Theology. Most
students judged it as very difficult. The professor was one of
the recognized scholars in the field of study, which is why it
was still open. Again, I thought, "What do I have to lose?" I
enjoyed the class from the very first day. I was studying the
meaning of things. I was learning things that I had previously
thought were too complex for me. Week by week, paper by
paper, I was getting a B, which, by the way, was the minimum
to stay in the program. One day, three weeks into the course, I
stayed after class to connect with the professor. "Do you know
who I am?" I asked. "Yes," he said, "You were the applicant
that we rejected. I was on the application review committee. I
read your whole application." After a long pause, I responded,
"Now that I have completed part of the course and have written
three papers what do you think?" He took a long pause and
looked me straight in the eye and said, "You're in! As head of
the committee I will write the acceptance letter." Wow, I was
in! What if the original rejection letter had caused me not to
go forward? Don't be surprised, but that three-year master's
degree took me seven years to complete. I experienced great
joy in taking that time to dig into the philosophical and theological meaning of life. I began applying it to everything and
everyone I encountered. Today I realize there was no way I
could have let that rejection letter stop me because the energy,
the grace of Divine Intent, pushed me forward when I needed
it the most. That is what Divine Intent is all about; we are given
strength to accomplish what we were created to do.

This is true in both the secular and the sacred dimensions
of life. Many of us believe the sacred came first, and then we

made it secular. If we surrender to the sacred parts of things first, secularism will right itself and all things will work for the good. (Even if we cannot see it at that moment in time.) The reason so few people can hear Divine Intent in their life is because they are too busy seeking tangible things of this world. These people frame their existence around the tangible dimensions: careers, houses, cars, boats, and stuff they feel will make them happy. They do not listen well, so they do not hear or understand the sacred dimension; they are not seeking the Divine Intent for their life. They speculate as to the answer of life and then take action based on their false understanding of their mere speculation. Whether you are listening to the person next to you or you are trying to listen to the Divine Intent, there is a pattern that is formed.

If you really want to come to know yourself:

1. Do not predetermine the goal of your life. Don't pick a career, a relationship, a neighborhood, and settle into it as the call of your life. Do not begin with an end in mind. Many people start by picking the goal and achieving it to only discover "it" was not the "it" they were meant to have. A saying attributed to St. Teresa of Avila states, "Be careful what you wish for because you might not enjoy the consequences!" Ted wanted to be a doctor because both of his parents were doctors. Perhaps it was not that Ted truly had a call to be a doctor, rather, he wanted to have the recognition and lifestyle a doctor has. He was really meant to be a teacher. I'm not talking about Ted specifically, but I have worked with a number of people like Ted who have made this mistake: they aren't called to the career; they want what the career offers.

2. Develop a list of questions that guide your listening. Remember, I made the point that great questions draw

great answers while poor questions render poor or no answers at all. Poor questions are usually "why" questions. Why did this happen to me? Why can't I do this? The better questions begin with "What?" What am I to learn from this? What is my Gift? What considerations do I need to entertain in order to connect with my Gift? How am I to relate to what is happening? What should I know that I do not know?

3. Look for convergent insights to your questioning. As you ask different questions the routine will bring you to similar answers. This is convergence, similar answers from different questions and different environments. In order to recognize the path, you must become a fervent listener. You must eliminate your skepticism or what is referred to as brainpower. Self-discovery is not about being smart. It is not about reasoning your way into a new reality. Let me say that self-discovery has nothing to do with new anything. It has everything to do with realities: who you truly are and what you have always been from the moment you were conceived. We all have a Divine path in our life. It is all about the "meant to be's." Most of us miss these "meant to be's" because we are consumed in the "I want to be's." We are so busy creating our own path or journey that we fail to open ourselves to the Divine way.

There is one thing that will keep you from an ever-deepening level of self-discovery; it is the human condition. The human condition has many innate habits that stall our journey. Most people never get detached enough from stuff to make room for insights, knowing Divine Intent. Their cup is full, and they have experienced many things that have not turned out the way they had planned. For the majority of people, what they get is not what they thought they would get, and they do not know what to do with what they got. This happens because they cannot detach themselves from their own desires. They fill their life with nonconvergent activity making them busy, yet ineffective. They get caught up in desiring what others have rather than what they are meant to have. They don't believe their journey is based on Divine Intent. They never move on from dreaming (reflecting,) into contemplation and action. They become outwardly focused, rather than inwardly reflective and actions are based on physical stimulation rather than self-understanding.

Another less obvious barrier to self-understanding is trying to think outside the box. Let's stop here for a moment. Over the past four decades there has been a trend referred to as "thinking outside of the box." This is based on the idea that thinking outside the box, thinking outside the situation, will give you some life-changing revelation. Organizational planners coined this as the thing, the swizzle stick, or the pet rock. They promote thinking outside the box to challenge lead organizations to get outside of themselves (their linear thought patterns). They proposed that this alone would change their thought pattern, stimulate creative thinking, and overnight, make their organization the leader in the market. This thesis is averse to what I have experienced. First, think inside the box, get to know your assets, liabilities, and Gift, and then take that self-understanding and apply it outside the box. If you know yourself from outside the box before you know the inside of the box, your self-understanding will never be any better than the environment, the job or relationship you happen to be in at the time. If the environment is positive and working, you will be positive and working. If the environment is negative and not working, your life will be negative and not working. The real objective is to have a life that is working even when the environment, job, or relationships are not working. The outside the box thinker never grows if the situation is not growing. The "inside the box" thinker finds good in every situation whether the situation is good or bad. Life does not get better because you get another job. Joy does not increase because you acquire something you have dreamed about nor does your self-image improve because you change relationships. You and your world will become better because you come to understand the uniqueness of you and learn to apply that uniqueness to what is already in your life.

Make a list of things you can do when you have joy. You see, joy is not about feeling joyful but rather a call to do something. It is about taking action when you are joyful. Action that generates joy will sustain the joy if the action is a part of Divine Intent in your life. How about calling someone you have had a conflict with to make amends? How about contributing a little of your time, your talent, and treasure when you have joy?

"Into your hands O Lord, I commend my spirit." (Psalm 31:5)